The Artist's Tools

by Stuart A. Kallen

LUCENT BOOKS

An imprint of Thomson Gale, a part of The Thomson Corporation

THOMSON

GALE™

702.8
KAL

Detroit • New York • San Francisco • New Haven, Conn. • Waterville, Maine • London

LIBRARY OF CONGRESS CATALOGING-IN-PUBLICATION DATA

Kallen, Stuart A., 1955–
  The artist's tools / by Stuart A. Kallen.
    p. cm. — (Eye on art)
  Includes bibliographical references and index.
  ISBN-13: 978-1-59018-957-3 (hardcover : alk. paper)
  ISBN-10: 1-59018-957-4 (hardcover : alk. paper)
  1. Artists' tools. I. Title. II. Series: Eye on art
  N8543.K35 2006
  702.8—dc22
                                                        2006017409

Printed in the United States of America

CONTENTS

Foreword

"Art has no other purpose than to brush aside . . . everything that veils reality from us in order to bring us face to face with reality itself."

—French philosopher Henri-Louis Bergson

Some thirty-one thousand years ago, early humans painted strikingly sophisticated images of horses, bison, rhinoceroses, bears, and other animals on the walls of a cave in southern France. The meaning of these elaborate pictures is unknown, although some experts speculate that they held ceremonial significance. Regardless of their intended purpose, the Chauvet-Pont-d'Arc cave paintings represent some of the first known expressions of the artistic impulse.

From the Paleolithic era to the present day, human beings have continued to create works of visual art. Artists have developed painting, drawing, sculpture, engraving, and many other techniques to produce visual representations of landscapes, the human form, religious and historical events, and countless other subjects. The artistic impulse also finds expression in glass, jewelry, and new forms inspired by new technology. Indeed, judging by humanity's prolific artistic output throughout history, one must conclude that the compulsion to produce art is an inherent aspect of being human, and the results are among humanity's greatest cultural achievements: masterpieces such as the architectural marvels of ancient Greece, Michelangelo's perfectly rendered statue *David*, Vincent van Gogh's visionary painting *Starry Night*, and endless other treasures.

The creative impulse serves many purposes for society. At its most basic level, art is a form of entertainment or the means for a satisfying or pleasant aesthetic experience. But art's true power lies not in its potential to entertain and delight but in its ability to enlighten, to reveal the truth, and by doing so to uplift the human spirit and transform the human race.

One of the primary functions of art has been to serve religion. For most of Western history, for example, artists were paid by the church to produce works with religious themes and subjects. Art was thus a tool to help human beings transcend mundane, secular reality and achieve spiritual enlightenment. One of the best-known, and largest-scale, examples of Christian religious art is the Sistine Chapel in the Vatican in Rome. In 1508 Pope Julius II commissioned Italian Renaissance artist Michelangelo to paint the chapel's vaulted ceiling, an area of 640 square yards (535 sq. m). Michelangelo spent four years on scaffolding, his neck craned, creating a panoramic fresco of some three hundred human figures. His paintings depict Old Testament prophets and heroes, sibyls of Greek mythology, and nine scenes from the Book of Genesis, including the Creation of Adam, the Fall of Adam and Eve from the Garden of Eden, and the Flood. The ceiling of the Sistine Chapel is considered one of the greatest works of Western art and has inspired the awe of countless Christian pilgrims and other religious seekers. As eighteenth-century German poet and author Johann Wolfgang von Goethe wrote, "Until you have seen this Sistine Chapel, you can have no adequate conception of what man is capable of."

In addition to inspiring religious fervor, art can serve as a force for social change. Artists are among the visionaries of any culture. As such, they often perceive injustice and wrongdoing and confront others by reflecting what they see in their work. One classic example of art as social commentary was created in May 1937, during the brutal Spanish civil war. On May 1 Spanish artist Pablo Picasso learned of the recent attack on the small Basque village of Guernica by German airplanes allied with fascist forces led by Francisco Franco. The German pilots had used the village for target practice, a three-hour bombing that killed sixteen hundred civilians. Picasso, living in Paris, channeled his outrage over the massacre into his painting *Guernica,* a black, white, and gray mural that depicts dismembered animals and fractured human figures whose faces are contorted in agonized expressions. Initially, critics and the public condemned the painting as an incoherent hodgepodge, but the work soon came to be seen as a powerful antiwar statement and remains an iconic symbol of the violence and terror that dominated world events during the remainder of the twentieth century.

The impulse to create art—whether painting animals with crude pigments on a cave wall, sculpting a human form from marble, or commemorating human tragedy in a mural—thus serves many purposes. It offers an entertaining diversion, nourishes the imagination and the spirit, decorates and beautifies the world, and chronicles the age. But underlying all these functions is the desire to reveal that which is obscure—to illuminate, clarify, and perhaps ennoble. As Picasso himself stated, "The purpose of art is washing the dust of daily life off our souls."

The Eye on Art series is intended to assist readers in understanding the various roles of art in society. Each volume offers an in-depth exploration of a major artistic movement, medium, figure, or profession. All books in the series are beautifully illustrated with full-color photographs and diagrams. Riveting narrative, clear technical explanation, informative sidebars, fully documented quotes, a bibliography, and a thorough index all provide excellent starting points for research and discussion. With these features, the Eye on Art series is a useful introduction to the world of art—a world that can offer both insight and inspiration.

Introduction

Tools of Creativity

People have been expressing themselves creatively for tens of thousands of years. From the twenty-thousand-year-old cave paintings in Lascaux, France, to the latest digital art burned onto a DVD, artists have relied on countless tools to produce lasting works of beauty and significance. Some modern-day tools, such as charcoal, brushes, and paints, are little different from those that might have been found in Italian painter Leonardo da Vinci's studio in the fifteenth century. Other tools, such as computers, have been used for art only since the early 1970s.

Whether made with traditional tools or modern machines, the visual arts include drawing, painting, ceramics, glass, sculpture, photography, and digital art. Each discipline requires the artist to use a variety of tools. Some tools may be homemade or improvised; others can cost thousands of dollars. Whatever their value or origins, the tools of creation, it is often said, are nearly as important as the talent of the artist who is using them. As internationally acclaimed artist, lecturer, and conservator Ralph Mayer writes in *The Artist's Handbook of Materials and Techniques:*

The artist studies his materials and methods in order to gain the greatest possible control over his manipulations, so that he may bring out the best characteristics of his chosen technique and express or convey his intentions properly, and in order to ensure the permanence of his results. Haphazard departure from approved methods will often involve a sacrifice in one of these directions, but those who have acquired a complete and intelligent grasp of [their tools] are usually able to vary the established procedures successfully, to suit their individual requirements.[1]

For the visual artist the choice of materials can have a lasting effect on the outcome of a piece of artwork. For example, a mediocre photograph can become a brilliant piece of art when chemically manipulated during the development

High-quality brushes such as these can help an artist execute his or her creative vision.

process. The choice of tools can have negative consequences as well. This might be seen when a beautiful painting fades, cracks, or fragments because it was painted with poor quality paint or created on cheap paper. For these reasons, those who want to avoid problems and make the best possible artwork must also learn to skillfully create or choose their tools and materials. This is not only beneficial to the artist but also increases the value of the artwork to collectors, galleries, and museums.

Tools Intertwined with Creation

The importance of artist's tools can be seen by how the materials themselves have influenced the very history of art. For example, when oil paints were developed in the fifteenth century, they were widely embraced by European painters during the Renaissance. The easy-to-use and permanent paints allowed painters to create masterpieces that were revered in their time and are considered priceless today. In the mid-nineteenth century the invention of the so-called French easel, a handy box that unfolded into a canvas holder as well as a palette, facilitated the new style of open-air painting. The easel and other inventions of

Some artists use modern tools such as infrared photographic film to help develop unique images.

the time, such as blunt-tip brushes, new, bright pigments, and portable paints sold in metal tubes were embraced by French impressionist painters. Claude Monet's unmatched paintings of water lilies, garden picnics, poppy fields, haystacks, and cathedral facades are testimony to the development of outdoor painting tools.

Similar trends may be seen when sculptors use power tools to create statues or when photographers use digital cameras to create photos that might be impossible with low-tech cameras. And the digital revolution has obviously influenced computer artists whose very work would not exist at all without the high-tech tools and software designed for its creation and display.

Whether an artist is creating a traditional-style painting in a manner developed five centuries ago or is working on a computer assembled last year, the tools are intertwined with the creation. Commenting on this phenomenon, American sculptor and art educator Lew Alquist wryly states: "Not everything is art, but everything is art supplies."[2]

1

Drawing and Painting

Drawing and painting are universal arts that have been practiced by both amateurs and professionals for thousands of years. Artistic expression is held in high esteem in most cultures, and paintings from ancient Egypt, China, Greece, Renaissance Europe, and elsewhere provide some of the most stunning visual records of the way people lived in the distant past. A few select paintings are some of the most valued objects on Earth. For example, in 2004 Pablo Picasso's painting *Boy with a Pipe* sold at auction for $104 million.

While paintings by famous artists are widely valued, most artwork is appreciated only by a small audience. It matters little, however, if a drawing or painting was created by an amateur or Picasso, for both were created with materials and tools that can be divided into three categories. The first category, the media, comprises the substances used to create the artistic design or image, such as pencil or graphite, ink, pigments, charcoal, and varieties of paint, including oils, acrylics, and watercolors. The second category comprises a variety of instruments artists use when applying the media. These tools include brushes, palettes, and the palette knife.

The third category—the substrate, support, or ground—comprises the surfaces to which the medium is applied and includes paper, wood, plaster, and canvas or other fabrics. Artists who make their own canvases also work with a variety of carpenter's tools to build frames over which they stretch and attach substrates such as linen, cardboard, or synthetic fabrics.

The Oldest Media

Long before the existence of canvas, paper, and fabrics, prehistoric artists burned sticks in fires to make charcoal, the oldest medium known, and used it to draw bison and reindeer on cave walls. Cave dwellers did not understand that burning wood changed the atomic structure of the carbon in the wood to the soft, unstructured form now known as charcoal, but they certainly recognized burned wood's ability to make lasting black lines and smudges. In the millennia that followed, charcoal has been used not only as an end medium in drawing but also as a preliminary medium for sketching images on panels or walls prior to painting.

In 2004, Pablo Picasso's *Boy with a Pipe* sold at auction for $104 million.

Compressed charcoal is a versatile medium used by beginners and skilled artists alike.

The materials and processes for manufacturing charcoal have changed little over the centuries. Since prehistoric times, artists have used many types of wood to make charcoal. However, contemporary artists prefer willow branches because the burned wood does not fragment during use. Charcoal made from vine branches is also appreciated because it produces a rich black color.

Artists can make their own charcoal using techniques described by Italian artist Cennino Cennini in 1437:

> Take a nice, dry, willow stick; and make some slips of it the length of the palm of your hand, or say four fingers. . . . [Smooth] them and sharpen them at each end, like spindles. Then tie them up in bunches . . . with a thin

copper wire. Then take a brand-new casserole, and put in enough of them to fill up the casserole. Then get a lid to cover it, [sealing] it with clay, so that nothing can evaporate. Go to the baker's in the evening, after they have stopped work, and put the casserole dish in the oven; and let it stand there until morning; and see wither these are well roasted.[3]

Today artists can heat the sticks in their own ovens rather than rely on the local baker. Most contemporary artists, however, take the simple step of purchasing charcoal at an art supply store.

Charcoal is produced in several forms. Charcoal sticks are pieces of vine, willow, or beech twigs that have been charred in special ovens called kilns. Compressed charcoal is charcoal dust mixed with a binder and pressed into sticks like pieces of chalk. Charcoal pencils are compressed charcoal encased in wood. These come in three grades: hard and medium for detail work, and soft for blending and smudging techniques.

Charcoal is an exceptionally versatile medium. It can be used by beginners who often need to erase and correct their drawings or by skilled artists who can use it for detailed figure drawings. As *The Artist's Manual*, edited by painter and art educator Angela Gair, states: "Charcoal is a wonderfully liberating medium, so immediate and responsive in use that it is almost like an extension of the artist's fingers. . . . Rich tonal effects, ranging from deep blacks to misty grays, are achieved by smudging and blending charcoal lines with the fingers."[4]

The Importance of Pigments

Artists who want to move beyond the simple black of charcoal must use pigments, substances that add color to paintings. Most pigments originate as finely powdered colored material. The earliest pigments were simply ground up earth or clay mixed with spit, fat, bone marrow, or even urine in order to make paint. Modern pigments are often sophisticated synthetic substances chemically engineered in laboratory settings. Whatever their source, pigments are an essential medium, as award-winning artist and educator Ray Smith writes in *New Artist's Handbook:* "Painting is the art of distributing pigment over the surface of a [support] and, as such, the particles of pigment, which provide the color for the work, are the single most important component in any consideration of the painting process."[5]

Many pigments chosen by the world's greatest artists have changed little over thousands of years. These substances are classified today as either organic or inorganic. Organic pigments, which contain carbon, come from vegetable or animal —that is, living—sources. Inorganic compounds do not contain carbon and are composed of minerals or chemical combinations of other elements.

Mark Sampson's charcoal drawing, *Red Ripe,* consists of many tones of black and gray.

The bright colors in Claude Monet's *The Artist's Garden at Vetheuil* were created with cadmium red and cadmium yellow paints.

The oldest inorganic pigments include a type of clay that contains iron and manganese oxides, which produce the yellowish brown color called sienna. Cinnabar, or vermilion, is a toxic mineral mix of mercury and sulfur that creates bright orange-red. Beginning around the sixth century, artists began grinding the semiprecious blue gemstone lapis lazuli into a fine powder to make ultramarine blue, while the mineral malachite was powdered to make a rich green pigment. Plants have also long been a source of pigments. Madder, for example, cultivated in Europe, Africa, Asia, and the Americas, is used to make the red pigment known as madder lake.

Pigments from animal sources are usually rarer and more unusual than those derived from plants, and few are still in use today. For example, the ink sac of cuttlefish or squid was at one time the source of the dark reddish brown color sepia. Another rare and unusual source of pigment was the bodily remains of Egyptian mummies, which made a dark brown color called mummy. One type of pigment, used to make the crimson color carmine, is made from the dried and pulverized bodies of the cochineal insect native to Mexico and South America. About 155,000 insects are required to make about 2.2 pounds (1kg) of this color, making the manufacture of insect-based crimson prohibitively expensive.

In the nineteenth century chemists discovered methods for creating pigments from metallic elements such as cobalt, chromium, zinc, manganese, magnesium, and titanium, adding a great variety of colors to the artist's palette. For example, around 1840 a complicated refining process involving acid solutions and hydrogen sulfide gas was used to make cadmium sulfide. This substance could be used to produce various shades ranging from very light yellow to deep orange and vibrant red. Cadmium orange was used to great effect by French impressionist Claude Monet in paintings such as *Haystacks* and *Water Lilies*. The bright spots of color in his *The Artist's Garden at Vetheuil* are attributed to cadmium red and cadmium yellow. Commenting on his preoccupation with these startlingly effective colors, Monet said, "Color is my day-long obsession, joy and torment."[6]

In the twentieth century, advances in chemistry allowed manufacturers to create pigments in nearly every color imaginable from petroleum compounds, acids, and other chemicals. Today there are over seven thousand pigments synthesized from petrochemicals and coal tars, with about two hundred new colors added each year. Most are used in printing inks, house paints, and colorants for textiles, plastics, automotive finishes, foods, and pharmaceuticals. Manufacturers of art paint buy what they need from the scraps and remnants of the industrial producers.

Pigments and Liquids

Pigments become paint, ink, or dye when mixed with oil, water, turpentine, or other fluids. These fluids are called vehicles. Natural vegetable oils such as walnut, sunflower, poppy, and linseed oil (extracted from flax seeds) are the main vehicles

Pastels are high-quality colored chalks that are used to create beautiful and lasting works of art. The following history of pastels was written by Flora Baldini Giffuni:

Technically, pastel is powdered pigment, rolled into round or square sticks and contained by methylcellulose, a non-greasy binder. It can either be blended with finger and stump [a kind of pencil consisting of a tight roll of paper or soft leather], or left with visible strokes and lines. Generally, the ground [support] is toned paper, but sanded boards and canvas are also popular. . . . When protected by fixative and glass, pastel is the most permanent of all media, for it never cracks, darkens or yellows.

Historically, its origin can be traced back to the Sixteenth Century, when . . . a galaxy of artists . . . used pastel as finished work, rather than for preliminary sketches.

Degas was the most prolific user of pastel, and . . . [his] protege, Mary Cassatt, introduced the Impressionists and pastel to her wealthy friends in Philadelphia and Washington. . . . Today, many of our most renowned living artists have distinguished themselves in pastels, and have enriched the world with this glorious medium.

Brightly colored pastel chalks have been used by some of the world's greatest artists to create lasting works of beauty.

Flora Baldini Giffuni, "About Pastels," Pastel Society of America, 2002. http://pastelsocietyofamerica.org/main/content/view/18/ 35.

used to make oil paints. Because of their viscous qualities, these oils allow the artist to control dispersion and blending of the pigments when applying them to the support.

Oils are called drying oils, incongruously, because they dry slowly—sometimes it takes years for the paints to set completely. Artists who want to speed up the drying process add a variety of resins called driers, or siccatives, to the paint. These include copal, a hard resin made from tree sap, and damar, a soft resin from the Hopea tree of Southeast Asia. Oil paints are favored by many artists, as Mayer explains:

> [Oil paint is superior because of its] great flexibility and ease of manipulation, and the wide range of varied effects that can be produced.
>
> [Oil paints give the artist] freedom to combine transparent and opaque effects, glaze and body color, in full range in the same painting.

Oil paints allow the artist to creatively blend colors.

> The fact that the colors do not change to any great extent on drying [means] the color the artist puts down is, with very slight variation, the color he or she wants. . . .
>
> [And the] universal acceptance of oil painting by artists and the public . . . has resulted in a universal availability of supplies, refined, developed, and standardized.[7]

Waterborne Media

Although many agree with Mayer about the superiority of oil paints, most painters also work with other media such as tempera paint, ink, acrylic paints, and watercolors. These are known as waterborne media because their pigments are mixed

Claude Monet's Impressionism

Impressionist painter Claude Monet (1840–1926) painted some of his most famous pictures in his garden in Giverny, France. The Foundation of Claude Monet at Giverny Web site details the painter's career:

[Claude Monet] spent his childhood and youth at Le Havre where, in the years between 1858 and 1862, he met the painters Eugene Boudin and [Johan] Jongkind, who introduced him to the pleasures of painting in the open air, directly from nature. . . . [Monet's] works were exhibited [beginning] in 1874 . . . alongside works by painters who were to be known as "impressionists," after an 1872 painting which Monet had entitled "Impression, soleil levant" [*Impression, Sunrise*]. . . .

[In 1883, Monet discovered the scenic beauty of Giverny where he] settled permanently. . . . He had flowers planted in his garden to enable him to paint in either fine or rainy weather. Every day he reproduced on his canvases the fields, the trees and the river Seine. . . .

It was at Giverny that he began his well-known "Series" which later made him famous. He painted the series of twenty-five "Haystacks" between 1888 and 1891 . . . and then the Japanese Bridge, Wistarias and Water Lilies with their interplay of sky, clouds, grass and flowers.

Foundation of Claude Monet at Giverny, "Claude Monet," 2006. www.fondation-monet.com/uk/ biographie/index.htm.

with water and various binders. The specific type of binder determines the nature of the paint. For example, egg yolks act as a binder for pigments in tempera paint, while shellac is the binder in ink. The binder in acrylic paint is polymer, a chemical compound similar to those used in plastic. Watercolor paints use gum arabic, a sap secreted by the acacia tree, as a binder.

The common characteristic of waterborne media is that the water evaporates after the paint is applied, and the binder holds the pigment to the support. Since water evaporates quickly, artwork made with waterborne media does not take long to dry and can be handled almost immediately. There are drawbacks to waterborne media, however. The artworks are less durable than those made with oil paints and can be damaged by humidity, pollution, handling, and storage.

Despite their ultimate impermanence, waterborne media artwork can last for centuries if handled properly. One of the oldest surviving watercolors, *A Young Hare* by German painter Albrecht Dürer, was created in 1502. Since that time some of the greatest painters, including Frenchman Paul Cézanne, the Swiss painter Paul Klee, and American painters Winslow Homer and Georgia O'Keeffe, have created masterpieces using watercolors.

Watercolors have also long been favored by aspiring artists because they are so easy to use. When mass-produced watercolors were first introduced in England in the late eighteenth century, thousands of people took up painting. The countless novices seen roaming the English countryside with their watercolor boxes tucked under their arms irritated professional artist Thomas Uwins. In a letter to a friend, he complained: "What a shoal of amateur artists we have got here. I am old enough to remember when . . . only [two] gentlemen condescended to take brush in hand, but now gentlemen painters rise up at every step and go nigh to push us off our [artist] stools."[8]

Renowned artists such as Paul Cézanne, Winslow Homer, and Georgia O'Keeffe have used watercolors to paint masterpieces.

Tempera Paint

Tempera paint, another waterborne media, is not as effortless to use as watercolor, but it is extremely durable and resistant to humidity, temperature changes, and darkening with age. Several tempera paintings made in the first century still survive. Artists originally created tempera by hand-grinding pow-

A Young Hare, painted by German painter Albrecht Dürer in 1502, is one of the oldest surviving watercolors.

dered pigments into egg yolk. Since the finished product was very brittle, artists diluted the egg with honey, water, powdered milk, or plant gums.

Tempera was first used by prehistoric artists and was the medium of choice before oil paints were developed. Even after oil paints came into fashion, many Renaissance artists continued to use tempera. Masterpieces made with tempera paints include Leonardo da Vinci's *Madonna and Child*, Michelangelo's *The Holy Family with the Infant St. John the Baptist*, and Sandro Botticelli's *The Adoration of the Magi*.

Acrylic Paints

Mediums such as tempera, oil, and watercolors have changed little over the centuries. However, in the late 1940s the introduction of acrylic paints created an entirely new style of painting. Acrylics are synthetic paints made with extremely fine particles of pigment suspended in acrylic polymer resin. This resin acts as a vehicle or binder when mixed with pigments. Because of their versatility and ease of use, the popularity of acrylic paints has come to rival that of oils since 1950. Acrylic paints dry quickly; are permanent; do not fade, darken, or yellow with age; adhere to any surface; and can be cleaned up with soap and water.

There are many complaints about acrylics despite the advantages of this medium. The main condemnation is explained in the saying: "The advantage of acrylic paint is that it dries quickly, but it has one disadvantage—it dries quickly."[9] This joke defines the problems artists encounter when working with acrylics. Their brushes dry fast and hard and must be kept in water when not in use. The paint also dries quickly on the palette unless it is sprayed continually with water. And, most problematic for some, the paint dries quickly on the support so that it cannot be manipulated and changed in the way oil paints can. However, those who like to paint quickly and apply successive layers of color without disturbing the underpainting have no problem with the fast-drying characteristic of acrylic paint. Since the 1950s a wide range of professional

Many artists like acrylic paints because they are permanent, quick drying, and can be cleaned up with soap and water.

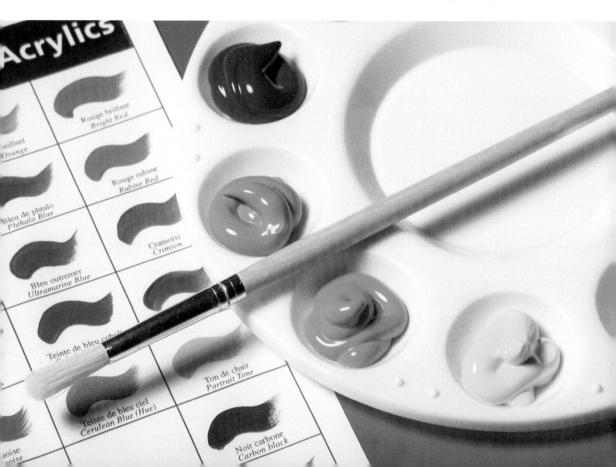

artists, including Ed Ruscha, Frank Stella, and Chuck Close, have produced lasting works using acrylic paint.

Brushes

Those who use acrylic paint often use synthetic-bristle brushes that have been developed specifically for the medium. Artists who work in oil or watercolor prefer natural-hair brushes. Whatever their medium, most artists agree that the role of the brush in painting is nearly as important as the paint itself. For this reason, paintbrushes are made from a wide variety of materials and come in many shapes and styles. Each type is meant to give the artist the utmost control over his or her work. As French impressionist Edgar Degas stated, "In a single brushstroke we can say more than a writer in a whole volume."[10]

The earliest painters used small bundles of twigs, palm fibers, or even their fingers to apply paint. By the sixteenth century brushes were made by professional brush makers who used the tail hairs of martens (called sables), badgers, mink, ermine, or squirrels (called camelhair). To make a brush, the brush maker snipped hairs from the very tip of the animal's tail and sorted them by length. The hairs were then inserted root down into the barrel of a quill—the hollow end of a feather, most often taken from waterfowl such as swans, geese, or ducks. For the final step the brush maker tightly clamped the hairs in the quill with a silver or copper wire called a ferrule. Brush assembly took great skill and required only the finest animal fur, making brushes very expensive.

In modern times good brushes remain costly since the sources of natural hair is diminishing as more species become endangered through trapping, climate change, and loss of habitat. The brushes most valued by artists are made from the hairs of several species of marten or weasel, including sable and Asian mink (called kolinsky).

Artists most prize red sable brushes because of their ability to hold a fine point and their spring—they quickly return to their natural shape. These brushes are expensive: In 2006 a medium-size red sable brush cost about $60. Kolinsky brushes are the most expensive and can cost up to $160.

More affordable alternatives are synthetic sable brushes, called white or golden sable, that cost about 10 percent of the price of a red sable brush. These are made from nylon filaments bundled together with a ferrule. Synthetic brushes are considered inferior by some painters because they have too much spring and the hairs are not as absorbent as those used in natural-hair brushes. Those who shun synthetic brushes but cannot afford sable can purchase brushes made from the hairs of the mongoose, squirrel, pony, ox (sabeline), or even monkey.

Rounds, Brights, and Filberts

Brushes differ not only in composition but also in size and shape. Artists choose specific brushes according to the type of medium they are using. For example, watercolor paints are light and watery, so they require a fine-quality brush that will perform well when absorbing the liquid paint. Oil painting brushes can be of lower quality, since the paint is viscous and does not easily drip from the brush.

Artists also choose specific brushes for different types of painting. For example, a round is a standard brush with a sharp tip that holds a lot of paint. Round brushes are used for general painting and blocking in the basic composition at the initial stage of creation.

A flat brush has square bristles used to cover large areas with paint, render edges, and apply paint with a minimum of texture. A bright brush also has a square pattern, but its hairs are about one-third the length of those in a flat. Brights are typically used when an artist wants to leave strongly textured brush marks in the paint or scrub paint onto a surface for a spe-

Flat brushes with square bristles are good for covering large areas without adding a lot of texture.

cial effect. Filbert brushes look like flats with rounded corners. These are used when an artist wants to blend colors, infuse soft edges, or create smooth textures with no visible brushstrokes. For fine detail work, artists use riggers—long, narrow brushes with flexible hairs.

Each type of brush is made in several sizes with numbers denoting the length and width of their hairs. The smallest brush is called a 000000 and the largest is a 24. The standard watercolor brush is a 7 round.

The Palette and Palette Knife

Not all artwork is the result of brushwork. Some artists use a palette knife to create works of art by applying oil paint to a canvas. Palette knives are also used to mix, scrape, or remove paint from a painter's palette.

Wooden hand-held palettes first came into use during the Renaissance, when oil paints grew in popularity. Originally, palettes were made from small, rectangular, paddle-shaped pieces of wood. By the 1800s oval or kidney-shaped palettes, with a center hole for the thumb, became popular with artists. To prevent oil paints from seeping into the wood, palette makers soaked the boards in linseed oil and allowed them to dry hard. In more recent times the thumb hole has been moved near the edge of the wood palette, and the surface is sealed with polyurethane varnish.

Not all artists prefer a wood palette, so some improvise and mix paints on sheets of marble, glass, or metal. Those who want to avoid cleanup use Styrofoam trays, paper plates, or thick sheets of paper or cardboard as disposable palettes.

The Painted Surface

Whether applied with a palette knife or brush, the end product of an artist's labor is the painted surface that holds the piece of art. Over the centuries artists have used a wide variety of grounds that include glass and stone; however, until the 1300s most paintings on rigid supports were painted on wood panels. The choice of wood was largely dictated by what grew

STRETCHING AND PRIMING CANVASES

*A*rtists can buy canvases that are prestretched or they can stretch their own, a task that requires skill. Artists who stretch canvases first need to buy the pieces that make the frame. These so-called stretcher bars are precut wooden sticks with slot-and-tendon joints that fit tightly together.

To stretch a canvas, the artist taps the stretcher bars together with a rubber mallet and uses a tape measure to make sure the frame is perfectly square. The canvas is cut with pinking shears and the frame is laid on top of the material. To attach the canvas, the artist pulls the edges of the fabric tight with canvas-straining pliers. The canvas is stapled to the bars with a heavy-duty stapler as the artist pulls it. After this is done, wooden wedges, or keys, are pounded into the joints of the stretcher bars to permanently hold the frame in place.

After the canvas is stretched it must be primed with a layer of gesso, a fine plaster made of gypsum that is mixed with animal-hide glue and painted onto the panel. This final step creates a surface that helps bind the paint to the fabric.

most abundantly in a particular region. The ancient Egyptians, for example, used cedar panels, some of which are preserved today. In Europe painters mostly used oak, but some also painted on lime, beech, chestnut, and walnut boards. One of the world's most famous paintings, da Vinci's *Mona Lisa*, was painted on poplar. Today, in addition to using traditional woods, artists create paintings on a type of extremely durable, lightweight fiberboard called Masonite.

Another common support, canvas, is a heavy woven fabric made from flax, hemp, linen, or cotton. A lightweight canvas stretched over a wooden frame has many advantages over a heavy wood panel, which can crack or damage the painted surface during handling. For this reason canvas became the most desirable support for artwork during the Renaissance. As *The Artist's Manual* states, canvas is "taut but flexible, and has a unique receptiveness to the stroke of the brush."[11]

Like other art materials, canvases are used by artists to create work that is unique. Although art has evolved significantly since the first cave dwellers smeared pigment on the walls of their shelters, the artist's work remains tied to the tools that are necessary to make a painting or drawing. There are few limits or rules, allowing artists to draw upon countless variations of pigments, paints, brushes, and supports to express a vision or preserve a moment. And long after the artist is gone, his or her creative voice may continue to speak through these materials to people in a far-distant time and place.

2

Tools of the Sculptor

Like painting and drawing, the art of sculpture is as old as humanity. Prehistoric sculptors fashioned small statues, or statuettes, from clay or carved them from wood, ivory, or soft stone such as soapstone. One of the oldest surviving stone sculptures, the Venus of Berekhat Ram, which was found in present-day Israel, resembles a female figure. This 230,000-year-old statuette is believed to have been carved by *Homo erectus*, the ancestor of modern humans. Other Venus figurines, which resemble heavily pregnant women, are more recent. One of the most well-known examples, the Venus of Willendorf, found in Austria in 1908, was carved from limestone around 24,000 B.C.

Since the first civilizations were founded around 9000 B.C. sculpture has remained an important art form in nearly every society. In 2900 B.C. the ancient Egyptians created giant sculptures such as the sphinx, a statue 60 feet (18.2m) high and 240 feet (73m) long with the body of a lion and the head of a man.

Today there are hundreds of thousands of sculptures in parks, museums, and public spaces throughout the world. Many of these statues are based on styles and techniques established in ancient Greece around the seventh century B.C. At that time sculptors began carving statues of young, athletic male and full-bodied female nudes with realistic features and strong character reflected in their faces.

Three-Dimensional Art

The word "sculpture" originated in Rome nearly three thousand years ago, and the Latin word *sculptura* means carved or cut out of stone. In its original usage the term likely referred only to objects that were carved from granite, marble, and other stones. In the centuries that followed, however, it came to be more inclusive and included works cut or carved from wood, clay, metal, bone, horn, wax, and other materials. Since the early twentieth century the definition of sculpture has become even more inclusive as sculptors created art from new materials such as glass, sand, liquid crystals, and plastic.

This Venus sculpture, found in 1908 in Willendorf, Austria, was carved from limestone around 24,000 B.C.

Although new types of material have been added over time, the basic definition of sculpture has not. According to artist and author Jack C. Rich in *The Materials and Methods of Sculpture*, "Sculpture is, essentially, a three-dimensional art concerned with the organization of masses or volumes. The sculptor composes his work in terms of volumes or masses, planes, contours, light and dark areas, and textures."[12]

Because of the many parameters that define a sculpture, some consider sculpting to be among the most difficult of arts. As Italian sculptor Benvenuto Cellini wrote in 1547: "I say that the art of sculpture is eight times as great as any other art based on drawing, because a statue has eight views and they must all be equally well made."[13]

An artist uses a chisel to add fine details to a wood sculpture.

Carving Wood

Sculptors can use a wide variety of materials while attempting to live up to Cellini's ideals. One of the easiest to work with is wood, which has many favorable qualities for use in sculpture. It is abundant and inexpensive, relatively light and easy to shape, and yet incredibly durable if painted or stained. There are many types of wood, and each has its own artistic virtues, including color, grain pattern, and degree of hardness. For example, finished mahogany is a warm reddish brown with a fine grain that gives it a silky smooth appearance. Bird's-eye maple has a rich ornamental grain pattern and is light brown in color. Rosewood is durable with a pleasant scent and a deep red color that may be streaked with yellow or black. Walnut is considered among the finest sculpture woods because its extreme hardness allows sculptors to create intricate details without fear of splintering the piece.

Sculptors who wish to carve wood can do so with a relatively simple set of woodworking tools. Hatchets, handsaws, and blades mounted on handles, called draw knives, are useful for the initial shaping of rough pieces of wood. The chisel and chisel-like gouges can be used to create finer details when either pushed through small pieces of wood by hand or tapped with wooden, metal, or rubber mallets. Rasps and files shred and sand details into the wood, while sandpaper and sanding blocks can be used to add a fine finish to a sculpture.

In regions such as New Zealand and the islands of Oceania, indigenous wood-carvers can create incredibly detailed pieces with a single instrument, the adz. This axlike tool has a curved blade that is extremely versatile. According to sculptor Oliver Andrews in *Living Materials: A Sculptor's Handbook*, "The adz combines the weight and handle of the

This Inuit woodworker's handmade toolbox (top), adz (center), and curved knife (bottom), could be used for carving large logs or embellishing small pieces with fine details.

mallet with the cutting edge of the chisel. It is unsurpassed for carving large logs and timbers. All the wood carving of Pacific Oceania is done with adzes, from the hollowing out of a fifty-foot canoe to the smallest detail on a paddle handle or ceremonial staff."[14]

Those who lack the adz skills of the Oceanians often rely on power tools to shape their pieces. Today most wood sculpture is created with table saws, drills, joiners, planers, routers, belt sanders, and even chain saws. These tools allow an artist to create a sculpture quickly and efficiently.

Whatever the tools in use, wood sculptures can be created from one or more pieces of wood. These may be attached to each other with an assortment of glues and metal fasteners such as bolts, screws, and nails. Finally, most wood needs to be finished so that it is preserved. Traditional sculptors coat their pieces with animal fat, wax, linseed oil, or paint. Others prefer synthetic wood preservatives such as polyurethane to add lasting permanence to a wood sculpture.

Stone Carving

Chisels, mallets, and power tools may also be found in the studios of sculptors who carve granite, marble, limestone, sandstone, onyx, alabaster, and other types of stone. Because of stone's extreme hardness, working with it requires great patience and skill. Despite the difficulties, however, sculptors have been carving rock for countless millennia.

The oldest stone-carving method involves hitting, scratching, rubbing, or chipping a soft stone with a harder one. The work of the sculptor was eased considerably in the eighth century B.C. when hardened iron tools were developed. Since that time the basic tools for creating stone sculptures have changed little.

There are three basic types of tools used for stone carving. Percussion tools are used to hit other tools or the stone itself. These include iron hammers and mallets, picks, axes, and adzes. Various cutting tools include toothed chisels, straight chisels, claw chisels, and sharp, narrow, pointed chisels called points. Stone sculptors also use a variety of abrasives to erode

the stone. These include drills, saws, grinding and cutting wheels, extremely hard sandpaper made from Carborundum, and water erosion machinery that sprays a high-powered, concentrated jet of water onto the sculpture. Many stone sculptors also rely on modern power tools such as pneumatic chisels and cutters, electric hammers, stone saws with diamond-tipped blades, sanders, and drills.

This stone sculptor wields a mallet and chisel with extreme patience and skill.

Plaster Casting

Not all sculptures are carved, and the process of casting makes it possible for an artist to create numerous identical sculptures from a single piece. Casting requires the creation of a mold, sometimes called a negative or mother mold, that is filled with liquid sculpture materials such as plaster, plastic, concrete, or molten metals such as bronze, a copper-tin alloy. The mold itself may be built from various materials including wax, glue, latex rubber, fiberglass, or sand. The most common mold material is plaster, and creating sculptures with this type of mold is called plaster casting, an extremely complicated and

MODELING CLAY

Sculptors who wish to make sketches or models can work with modeling clay, a nonhardening substance that is extremely plastic, or workable. Michael Delahunt explains the characteristics of modeling clay:

[Modeling clay] cannot be used for permanent work (unlike ceramic water-based clays, it is never fired or glazed). Although it becomes less useful as its oil either dries or is absorbed from it (making it brittle) or as it picks up impurities, . . . it can be reused for many years if kept relatively clean. Even new it can vary greatly in quality. Most common varieties are made of clay mixed with petroleum greases, oils (typically linseed oil), turpentine, sulfur dioxide, and pigments. It softens as it is modeled by the hands (because of their warmth), [and] pieces [can be] joined to each other by pressing them together and blending with fingertips. Equipment that might be used with modeling clay includes modeling tools and armatures.

Michael Delahunt, *Artlex Art Dictionary*, March 4, 2006. www.artlex.com.

labor-intensive procedure that requires the artist to successfully complete many steps.

To begin plaster casting, an artist creates an original model, usually from clay. Once this step is completed, the sculptor makes a wooden mold box or some other outer shell that can hold the original model in place. The original model is coated with a lubricant such as petroleum jelly, so that the plaster will not stick to it. Thin brass plates, called shims, are stuck into the original, sunk about 1/4 inch (6mm) into the clay. The shims will divide the mold in half so that it can be separated into two pieces when it dries. A more complicated art piece, such as a soldier riding a horse, requires the sculptor to make a mold from more than two pieces.

After securing the original in the mold box the artist mixes plaster to a creamy consistency in a bucket and pours it into the mold. When the plaster hardens, the mold is disassembled at the shims and the original is removed.

To cast a new sculpture, the details of the original now outlined in the plaster, called the interface, must be coated with petroleum jelly or wax and the mold must be reassembled. Artists making plaster or concrete sculptures mix the liquid and pour it into the mold. After it is dry, the mold is separated and the sculpture is removed. Oftentimes the finished work shows the seams of the mold and these need to be sanded out with sandpaper or an electric sander. The final work may be coated with paint, glaze, or other finishes.

Metal Casting

Sculptors who wish to cast bronze or other metals practice an ancient skill first developed by the Chinese around 3000 B.C. By the seventh century B.C. the Greeks were using this procedure to produce thousands of bronze statues, many of which survive today. However, by the late eighteenth century, casting had become an industrial process practiced on a large scale to produce machinery and cheap consumer goods. Artists were replaced by foundry workers and the process came to be considered esoteric and extremely difficult, as Andrews explains:

> During the nineteenth and first half of the twentieth century it was assumed that artistic bronze casting was a skill of baffling complexity and delicacy, which could be practiced only by craftsmen trained for generations at their inherited trade. The casting of bronze,

This bronze sculpture was created by a Chinese artist as early as 1,000 A.D.

iron, and aluminum was, of course, practiced regularly in industry, but these manufacturing processes were thought to be too cumbersome and technically awesome for an artist to carry out in a studio.[15]

In the 1950s this situation began to change when sculptors experimented with small homemade foundries and rejuvenated an ancient process called lost wax casting.

Lost Wax Casting

Lost wax casting relies on the creation of a wax sculpture that is used as an original model. To initiate this process, the artist must make an original piece of art from clay or another substance and then make a plaster mold of it like the molds used in plaster casting. Next, wax—which is sold by weight in long rods, slabs, or blocks—is liquefied in professional melting tanks that can heat 300 pounds (136 kg) of wax at a time. Artists making smaller sculptures can chip off small pieces of wax with hammers and chisels and melt it in kitchen or restaurant equipment such as pots or electric cooking appliances.

Once liquefied, the molten wax is poured into the mold and allowed to harden. The resulting wax model is an exact duplicate of the original work. After the wax solidifies, the mold is removed and the model is redetailed, or chased. This process is accomplished with knives, sanders, soldering irons with various tips, and propane torches. Whatever the tools, the point of chasing is to refine the wax model to its most perfect form.

Once the model is detailed, another mold is built up around it. To make a small sculpture, the sculptor might place the wax model into an empty juice can or piece of stovepipe. A bigger model may be placed in a large steel drum or a fabricated metal container. Whatever the case, the model is secured inside the container and metal tubes, called gates, are fitted around the model so that molten bronze can later be poured evenly throughout the mold. Other tubes, called vents, are inserted to let the hot gases of the molten metal escape. Finally, the sculptor mixes an investment liquid of water, silica flour, and plaster and pours it over the model.

METALWORKING

*A*lthough casting is the oldest method used to produce sculptures, modern industrial technology allows artists to create metal pieces through forming and welding. Sculptors who wish to perform metalwork assemble tools similar to those used by industrial manufacturers. These include hacksaws, drills, chisels, hammers, files, metal shears, wrenches, pipe benders, and folders. They also include electric or hydraulic tools such as band saws, press brake folders, grinders, and drill presses that can shape large pieces of sheet metal and iron rods. Arc welders and oxy-acetylene cutting and welding tools are also available to sculptors who wish to cut and join metal pieces.

Metalworking with these tools became popular with many young sculptors after World War II, as Oliver Andrews explains:

> Perhaps this had something to do with the usefulness of welding in salvaging the broken debris of an industrial society and forming it into shapes with new meanings. In any case, by the mid-fifties every art school with a sculpture studio had to have a welding torch, and junkyards and dumps were yielding their rusted treasures to be resurrected as art.

An oxy-acetylene torch allows an artist to create a modern sculpture from industrial debris.

Oliver Andrews, *Living Materials: A Sculptor's Handbook.* Berkeley and Los Angeles: University of California Press, 1983, p. 221.

After the investment liquid has hardened, the sculptor places the mold into a kiln, gradually heating the mold to 250°F (121°C). This process, called the burnout, causes the wax model to melt and run out of the mold, hence the name lost wax casting. The mold is left in the kiln and the temperature is slowly raised to 1,100°F (593°C) and held there for twelve to thirty-six hours. This hardens the mold sufficiently to receive the molten bronze without cracking.

While the mold is firing, the sculptor prepares the bronze. This requires a propane-fired crucible furnace, usually built from concrete and specially hardened fire brick. The center of the furnace holds a heavy graphite or porcelain cup called a crucible, where bronze ingots, or bars, are melted.

After the ingots have liquefied at 2100°F (1148°C) several people are required to perform what is called the "Dance of the Pour."[16] The ceramic mold is removed from the kiln and the

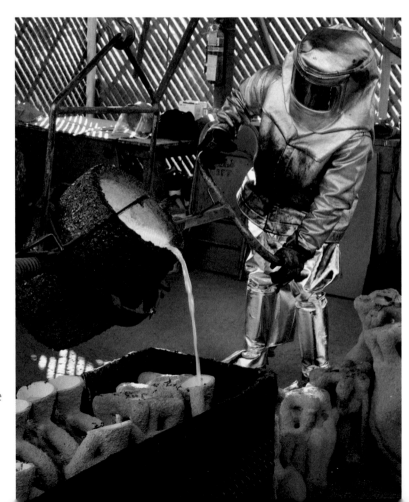

An artist performs the "Dance of the Pour," creating multiple sculptures by pouring molten metal from a crucible into several molds.

crucible is lifted from the furnace either by long tongs with extended handles, or a crane. The artisans engaged in this act are exposed to toxic fumes and the possibility of extreme burns while handling the molten metal. Although they wear respirators and protective gloves, boots, goggles, and headgear, it is still a very hazardous job. For this reason, the artisan assigned the task of guiding the crucible over the mold is called the "deadman."[17]

The pour of the molten metal into the mold is performed quickly. Once this crucial step is done, the filled mold is removed to a sandpit. When it cools enough to be handled, the plaster is chipped off, or divested, with a hammer and chisel or small pneumatic jackhammer. After the largest pieces are divested, the remaining plaster is removed with a sandblaster, or wire brush or by soaking in a mild sulfuric acid solution. The gates and vents are cut away with a power saw or arc welder. The welder may also be used to fill in holes or depressions in the sculpture, which is now finished in a rough form.

The final sculpture is finished smooth with a sandblaster, welder, and various sanding tools. The piece may then be hand polished and covered with a patina, a colored coating produced by treatment with various chemicals. Three compounds form the basis for most patinas: Ferric nitrate produces reds and browns, cupric nitrate creates greens and blues, and sulphurated potash produces black. After patination, the sculpture is waxed to a lustrous shine and mounted on a heavy base, usually made of marble.

Although lost wax casting is complicated, dangerous, expensive, and time consuming, it produces sculptures that are finely detailed and nearly indestructible. As Andrews writes, "It's amazing how well preserved are some of the bronzes that have lain for centuries in the earth or under the sea."[18]

Plastic and Fiberglass

Since the 1950s sculptors have been working with a material that is nearly as long-lasting and weather-resistant as bronze but much easier to cast and sculpt. The term "plastics," or synthetic

Polymer resins and tints pictured here can be formed into a wide variety of shapes and textures.

polymers, refers to a wide variety of materials such as acrylic, nylon, silicone rubber, polyethylene, polystyrene, vinyl, silicone, polyester, and at least fifty other substances. Many of these materials are used to make common objects, such as computer cases, automobiles, clothing, toys, furniture, and countless other products.

Artists select plastics depending on the type of work they want to create, since the materials have many different colors and textures. Plastics may be hard or soft; transparent, translucent, or colored; solid, liquid, fiber, foam, or adhesive. Artists can use these materials to carve, cast, or press a sculpture into a specific shape.

While artists create works from a wide range of plastic material, polyester resins are among the most common plastics used in artwork. This material is strong, lightweight, nearly impervious to weather, and can be used to create an infinite variety of colors, shapes, and textures.

Artists working with polyester begin their work with a thick liquid called polyester resin. This liquid hardens over the course of thirty minutes when mixed with a substance called a catalyst. Polyester is highly toxic in its liquid state and sculptors who work with resins must wear protective clothing such as rubber gloves, goggles or face shields, and respirators. Many also invest in industrial fans to clear the studio air of fumes. Although working with noxious polyester resin can be difficult, pouring the substance from a container into a mold is a much simpler process than heating metal to several hundred degrees. After casting a sculpture from polyester, the final product can be easily chased either with the solvent acetone or sandpaper and small power tools.

Foam polystyrene, known by the trade name Styrofoam, is another common plastic used for sculpture. This material, which is sold in blocks, rods, boards, and sheets, is easily cut with hand saws, rasps, electric carving knives, soldering irons, or welding torches. Unlike those made from polyester, sculptures made from plastic foam are not permanent. Therefore, Styrofoam is often used as the core material in a sculpture that is coated with concrete, plaster, or fiberglass (polyester resin

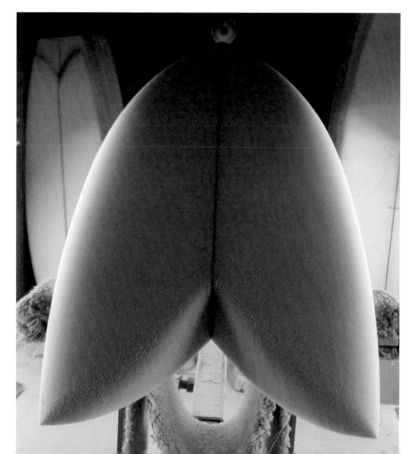

This modern surfboard is a sculpture shaped from polyurethane foam.

THE UNIQUE SCULPTURES OF EVA HESSE

Sculptor Eva Hesse is known for her use of unusual materials, such as fiberglass and latex. The following biography is provided by the Guggenheim Museum's Web site:

Eva Hesse was born January 11, 1936, in Hamburg. Her family fled the Nazis and arrived in New York in 1939. . . . When Hesse was ten years old, her mother committed suicide. Racked with anxiety throughout most of her life, Hesse nonetheless persevered in her single-minded pursuit of making art. . . .

In 1961, Hesse was included in group exhibitions at the Brooklyn Museum and at the John Heller Gallery, New York. That year . . . [she] made her first three-dimensional object—a costume made of chicken wire and soft jersey. . . .

Hesse began to use latex to make sculpture in 1967, and then fiberglass the following year. She started to gain recognition by the late 1960s, with solo shows . . . and inclusion in many important group exhibitions. While Hesse's work shows affinities with the concerns of Minimalism, it cannot be easily characterized under any particular art movement. . . . In 1969, [Hesse] was diagnosed with a brain tumor, and after three operations within a year, she died May 29, 1970.

Sculptor Eva Hesse peers through one of her sculptures made from rubber-coated string and rope.

Guggenheim Museum, "Eva Hesse: Biography," 2006. www.guggenheimcollection.org/site/artist_bio_63.html.

mixed with glass fibers). To create a sculpture core from Styrofoam, artists may construct a piece using glue, nails, and screws.

There are many examples of plastic sculptures in museums and public plazas. Eva Hesse is known for her fiberglass sculptures, such as *Sans II*, displayed in the Whitney Museum of American Art in New York, and *Repetition 19, III*, in the Museum of Modern Art in New York. The Walker Art Center in Minneapolis displays a diverse array of plastic sculptures, including Claes Oldenburg's *Three-Way Plug*, made from vinyl and polyurethane foam, and Joep van Lieshout's *The Good, the Bad, and the Ugly*, created from wood, steel, polyurethane, fiberglass, plastic, and bronze.

Both used alone and with other materials, plastic has revolutionized the art of sculpting. Although the material is most often recognized for its ubiquity in daily life—and its impact on the environment—it can also be crafted to preserve a moment in time or create a unique vision. But no matter whether an artist uses plastic, wood, metal, plaster, or wax, sculpting is an art form that requires precision tools wielded with skill and determination. And judging from the great number of statues in parks, museums, public buildings, and private yards, there is no shortage of artists willing to perform often formidable feats with malleable materials in order to fill the demand for sculptures.

Ceramics and Glass

Simple products of the earth can be processed into beautiful works of art that last thousands of years. Chinese porcelain pottery more than thirty-five hundred years old is made from clay and mineral glaze, a glasslike substance used for coating and decoration. In Egypt, samples of glass from the sixteenth century B.C. have been found that were produced from sand, lime, and wood ash. Whether ceramic or glass, these pieces have survived because their basic elements were exposed to high temperatures for extended periods of time. The extreme heat transformed the elements and fused them into a rock-hard permanence that has endured for millennia.

Ceramics are among the oldest artworks ever found and are common to ancient cultures from Egypt, Asia, Europe, Oceania, and the Americas. Some ceramics, such as bowls and cups, were used for eating, cleaning, and other daily activities. Others, such as figures of gods and goddesses, were created to serve as religious icons. Antique ceramics such as painted porcelain were valued as works of art. In modern times artists have created all manner of artwork from ceramics, including beautiful boxes, teapots, plates, busts, human figures, and abstract pieces such as Picasso's *Centaur*. What most of these pieces have in common are the intricate and colorful glaze patterns that the artists have painted onto these works.

Earthenware

"Ceramic" is a broad term used to describe items made from fired clay, and these objects are divided into three categories: earthenware, stoneware, and porcelain. Each group is distinguished by the mineral content of the clay and glazes and by the kiln temperature at which it is fired.

Earthenware, used for tableware and decorative objects, is made from four elements blended in various proportions by the artist. Artists who create earthenware mix a material that is about one quarter standard pottery clay and one quarter soft, white clay called kaolin, which is 98 percent free from

Pablo Picasso created this sculpture, *Centaur*, from bronze in 1948.

impurities. Another 35 percent of earthenware is mineral quartz, and about 15 percent is the mineral feldspar. Earthenware is fired in a kiln at a relatively low temperature, 1800° to 2100°F (1000° to 1150°C). Unglazed earthenware, because of its porous state, is not suitable for holding liquids, which will be absorbed into the clay. This problem is remedied if the piece is glazed in a second firing.

Earthenware has a variety of names, depending on its clay composition, color, or city of origin. Terra-cotta is an ancient form of earthenware made from a red clay and lightly fired. Delftware is blue and white pottery first created in the town of Delft, Netherlands, in the 1700s. Creamware, created in England in 1750, is a cream-colored product with a transparent lead glaze made of white clay from Devon. When it was first made by famed ceramics maker Josiah Wedgwood it was very popular with Charlotte, the wife of King George III. As a result the pieces came to be called Queen's ware.

A ceramic piece placed atop burning straw will develop the unique pattern of cracks and discolorations found on raku pottery.

Raku is a type of Japanese pottery developed around 1525 that is fired at low temperatures. Traditionally, raku pieces are removed from the kiln while red-hot and plunged into water. In recent decades Western ceramists developed a technique in which a raku piece is placed into combustible material such as sawdust, newspaper, or straw. Both methods cause unpredictable cracks and discoloration in the glaze that makes each raku piece unique.

Stoneware

Stoneware is stronger, more durable, and less porous than earthenware. This material, which is considered human-made stone, achieves its tough properties because it is fired at a higher heat than earthenware—between 2280° and 2370°F (1250° and 1300°C). At this temperature the clay begins to vitrify—that is, melt or fuse together into a glasslike substance. Vitrification makes stoneware resistant to liquids without glazing although artists often glaze it for decorative purposes.

Stoneware has been produced in China for thousands of years, and examples of stoneware pots in Europe date to the twelfth century. In the 1670s John Dwight made the first stoneware jugs and mugs in England and, after achieving success, created prized figurines and portrait busts from the material. Like earthenware, varieties of stoneware are named for their color or place of origin. These styles include brown stoneware, black basaltes, Elers redware, and Nottingham stoneware.

Porcelain

The hardest form of ceramic is called porcelain. First created in China between A.D. 600 and 900, porcelain is often referred to as china no matter where it was produced. Porcelain is defined by its fine white color, a result of a higher proportion of kaolin clay. Porcelain's hard texture and translucent quality are a result of vitrification that occurs at temperatures over 2480°F (1360°C).

Porcelain has qualities that make it useful for many products. Because it resists electricity, it is used for insulating material on power lines. Because it is durable and white, is has been used to make false teeth. For artists, porcelain's delicate beauty makes it the ideal material for making plates, cups, sculptures, statues, vases, and other decorative pieces.

"The Expressive Gesture"

Artists who create pieces from porcelain, stoneware, or earthenware use similar skills, tools, and equipment. Clay, a natural product of the earth, is at the heart of every ceramic piece. Sculptors classify clay as extremely malleable, or plastic, a term that in this sense means capable of being shaped or formed.

This vase, which sold for more than $14 million, is an excellent example of the delicate beauty found in ancient Chinese porcelain.

Water-based clay is very flexible when wet. For this reason, according to Andrews, clay "is unsurpassed for recording the expressive gesture of the human hand."[19]

Clay is formed by erosion, flowing rivers, and decaying vegetable matter and mold. Some artists prefer to dig their own clay with shovels and buckets, searching for deposits with uniform body, fine grain, and few impurities. This material is bluish to green in color due to the mold content, which also gives the substance a pungent odor and slippery feel.

Raw clay needs to be processed to remove impurities. To do so, the clay is soaked in water until it becomes a thick, viscous liquid called slurry. This is poured through a series of sieves, each with a progressively finer mesh, that strain out rocks, weeds, sticks, and other foreign debris. The slurry is then poured into a piece of cloth, often the leg of an old pair of jeans with a knot tied at the bottom, to allow the water to drain. After several days the clay achieves proper working consistency.

Most artists forgo the laborious process of digging their own clay by purchasing it from art material dealers. The clay is usually sold in 50-pound (23kg) cartons, which in 2006 cost about fifteen to twenty dollars each, depending on quality. Because of the cost of shipping such heavy packages, some artists buy powdered clay, which can be mixed with water in the studio. Whether powdered or wet, there are several types of clay, including terra-cotta, white China kaolin, and versa, so-named because it is extremely versatile and can be used for sculpting or ceramics.

Working with Clay

Artists who work with clay require a variety of tools, from the inexpensive and simple to the costly and complex. Before it can be used, clay has to be kneaded like bread and pounded against a plaster slab called a wedging table. This handwork, called pugging, softens and blends the clay and allows the sculptor to mix in a conditioner called grog, made from clay that has been fired and ground into fine granules. Grog adds a gritty texture called "tooth" to pottery. It also reduces shrinkage and promotes even drying in the kiln while adding structural strength to the finished piece. If the artist is working with powdered clay, it needs to be pugged with water in large cans until it

A variety of sticks, cutters, and other tools like those pictured are used by potters to shape clay pieces.

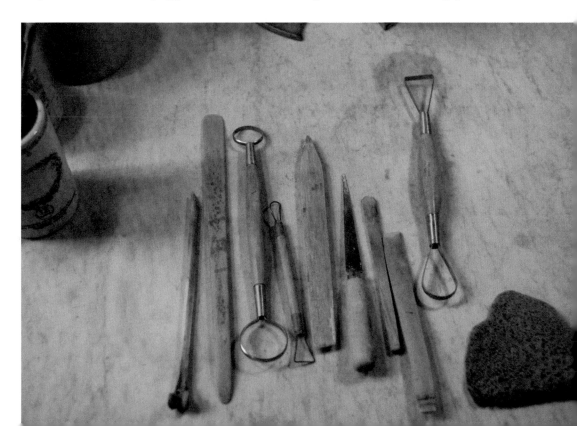

achieves the desired plasticity. After the clay is pugged unused portions are stored in bins that have airtight lids so that it will not dry out.

Because pugging is time-consuming and labor-intensive, an artist may purchase a pug mill. This machine has revolving blades that chop, mix, and deair, or remove the air bubbles from clay. (Air bubbles must be removed or the piece will explode in the kiln.) The pug mill can also be used to recycle partially dried clay by mixing it with moister matter.

Once the clay is ready for working, the artist slices off a desired portion with a knife or a slicing tool that utilizes a taut wire like a cheese cutter. If the piece is to be flattened, the artist may roll it out with a rolling pin or pound it with a wooden mallet.

The Pottery Wheel

After the clay is prepared it can be made into a sculpture or turned into a flowerpot, plate, bowl, cup, or decorative piece of artwork. Oftentimes this work is done on a pottery wheel that consists of several pieces. The wheelhead, a smoothly revolving circular platform capable of rotating at varying speeds, is where the artist places the ball of clay to begin the process. The wheelhead is turned by a pedal, flywheel, or some other device. The most basic pottery wheels operate on foot power—the potter uses his or her feet to rotate the wheelhead. Modern wheels are powered by electricity.

Aside from the pottery wheel, potters rely on their two hands to "throw a pot"—that is, to shape the ball of clay as it rapidly spins on the wheelhead. Through various hand techniques, potters open up a hole in the center of the clay, form it into a hollow cylinder, push out the center, make rims called collars, and finish the piece with a small strip of chamois leather to create a smooth rounded rim. Sometimes tools called throwing sticks are used to aid in this process. These tools are used to open and shape the clay vessel as it turns on the wheel. Some have specific purposes, such as forming the graceful angles of teacups.

After a piece is finished a potter may add handles, lips, lids, and other features. These are made with a variety of hole cutters, wood paddles, putty knives, kitchen knives, box cutters, and modeling knives with thin, sharp blades.

When a piece is finished it is allowed to partially dry into a malleable state called leather hard. At this point the artist can pare off imperfections with a knife or put the piece back on the wheel to reshape it. This may be done with tools that leave texture in clay. For example, small rolling pins called texture rollers leave parallel grooves in the clay. Wire brushes make a mottled surface. Clay stamps, like rubber stamps used with ink, can create intricate patterns when pushed down into the soft clay.

Not all ceramics are produced on a pottery wheel. Some artists cut slabs or sheets of clay to construct boxes and abstract artwork. This is often done with beveling tools that cut the edges of the clay at 30-, 45-, 60-, or 90-degree angles. Smaller pieces may be formed with a tile cutter, a mold like a cookie cutter that cuts square shapes from the clay.

The Kiln

After the piece of clay artwork is formed, it is fired for the first time, a process called bisque firing. This is done in a kiln that may be built in a variety of shapes and sizes. The earliest kilns were simply holes dug in the ground or cut into the sides of hills and were fueled with wood, coal, brush, or even cattle dung. Some traditionalist artists continue to use natural-style kilns today. However, modern kilns are gas- or electric-fired and range in size from small studio units to very large industrial ovens.

Most kilns can fire a number of pieces, and because of the energy expenses involved with running a kiln, artists tend to fire more than one piece at a time. For this reason kilns have mobile shelves, called kiln furniture, that can be loaded with clay pieces or removed if only a few pieces are being fired. The length of time the artwork remains in the kiln can be hours or days and depends on the size of the pieces. After the bisque firing is completed, the piece is ready for glazing.

This kiln, loaded with mobile shelves called kiln furniture, holds pottery that has been glaze fired.

Glaze Coating

Glazes are mixed from three basic elements. The first is a glass-forming agent, most commonly silica, a common element of sand. When exposed to temperatures of 1700°F (927°C) in a kiln during the glaze firing process, the silica is vitrified, or melted onto the piece. Because this extreme temperature might

UNIQUE METHODS AND TOOLS

In recent years modern ceramists have devised new and unique ways to combine clay and glazes. For example, potter, writer, and teacher Peter Pinnell believes that by adding texture to his work, he can convey the feeling that his pieces are special objects. Pinnell uses a bulb syringe filled with liquefied clay to create repetitive patterns on his teapots. To add a fuzzy or corroded look to a piece, Pinnell uses a small wiry bottle brush or toothbrush. Finally, a specially formulated glaze is sponged over the piece to give it a burnished-metal patina.

Jim Connell is a ceramist who believes in using unusual methods to fire pieces in the ancient raku process. Connell first creates pots using raku clay, which is more porous than stoneware clay. The pots are bisque fired then glaze fired in a kiln. When the pot is red-hot, Connell removes it from the kiln and quickly transfers it to a garbage can filled with crumpled newspaper. The heat of the pot ignites the newspaper into a fiery inferno as Connell quickly drops the lid on the can. After several hours, the pot is finished. Its glaze is uniquely cracked, bubbled, and oxidized in the traditional raku manner.

also melt clay, a second element of glaze called the fluxing agent is added. Fluxing agents make silica melt at lower temperatures and include lead, boron, sodium, and potassium. The third element of glaze, alumina, makes the other two ingredients more stable and viscous and thus prevents them from becoming too liquid and running off the piece.

Ceramists add other elements to glaze to create various opacities and colors. For example, tin creates an opaque white. Titanium dioxide creates a mottled effect by producing tiny white speckles. Iron is a common element used to create colors ranging from pale yellow to dark brown and black, depending on its proportion in the mix. Cobalt creates a blue glaze and copper generates colors from peacock green to bright reddish brown. Magnesium produces a dull purple or a bright violet when mixed with cobalt.

Glazes can also be formulated to create a variety of textures. For example, according to teacher and author Tony Birks in *The Complete Potter's Companion*, kaolin clay when added to a raw glaze "has a distinctive feel which an experienced potter can recognize blindfolded," while the mineral dolomite has a "crystalline, distinctly oatmealy look."[20]

Glaze ingredients consist of fine powders that are sold in bags. They are mixed with water and applied to clay pieces in a variety of ways. To create a uniform, single-colored piece, ceramists may use a pitcher to pour the glaze over the clay or use tongs to dip the piece in a tub filled with liquid glaze. Drips may be wiped away with a soft brush or small piece of sponge.

Other methods of applying glaze are limited only by the artist's imagination. Intricate patterns may be painted on with brushes. Abstract textures may be applied with a sponge or an old toothbrush, or sprayed on with a bulb syringe or air brush. Sometimes artists use a combination of several application methods to create a unique piece. Afterward, the piece is glaze fired, or fired for a second time. This final step transforms a simple piece of clay into a ceramic artwork, a process described by Birks:

> The naked pot is rather like a naked body. What attracts the eye is the form. . . . The color is more or less the same all over, all predictable. A layer of glaze is nicely described as "coating the body," for glaze clothes the pot. Glazes, like clothes, are both practical and an opportunity for display, satisfying for those who are excited by texture and color.[21]

Working with Glass

Like glaze, glass is a combination of three basic elements that are transformed by heat into unique and immortal works of art. When heated to 1830°F (1000°C), glass becomes viscous

and may be blown, stretched, colored, pulled into thin threads, flattened, or cast into sheets or blocks. When these pieces cool, they can be fused with other glass, cut, carved, sawed, drilled, etched, engraved, laminated, painted, and polished. Finished works of glass are unique in that they alter, diffuse, refract, reflect, or transmit light like no other work of art.

A potter dips newly made clay bowls in a yellow glaze.

The methods and tools for working with glass have changed little over the past two millennia. Glassblowers, called gaffers, need to melt glass ingredients into a molten form, cool the liquid several degrees, and either pour or blow the glass into a final form. To perform this hot, dangerous, and difficult work, gaffers must wear safety glasses, heat-resistant gloves and aprons, and other protective wear.

Gaffers begin by melting glass materials in a free-standing electric or gas-heated furnace called a pot furnace. At the center of the furnace one or more ceramic crucibles, or pots, are used to hold anywhere from 30 to 300 pounds (13.6 to 136k) of glass.

The crucible is filled with raw glass materials, called the batch. Each batch contains a glass recipe that is approximately

The modern interest in glass as art, known as the Studio Glass movement, began in 1962 when new techniques were devised to create glass on a small scale. The Studio Glass movement inspired one of its foremost practitioners, Dale Chihuly, to develop innovative techniques for producing artwork, as the following biography from Chihuly's Web site explains:

Dale Chihuly is most frequently lauded for revolutionizing the Studio Glass movement, by expanding its original premise of the solitary artist working in a studio environment to encompass the notion of collaborative teams and a division of labor within the creative process. However, Chihuly's contribution extends well beyond the boundaries of both this movement and even the field of glass: his achievements have influenced contemporary art in general. Chihuly's practice of using teams has led to the development of complex, multipart sculptures of dramatic beauty that place him in the leadership role of moving blown glass out of the confines of the small, precious object and into the realm of large-scale contemporary sculpture. In fact, Chihuly deserves credit for establishing the blown-glass form as an accepted vehicle for installation and environmental art, beginning in the late twentieth century and continuing today.

Davira S. Taragin, "Biography," Chihuly, 2002. www.chihuly.com/intro.html.

65 percent sand, 20 percent soda ash, and 15 percent limestone. These materials must be carefully weighed on a large industrial scale to produce the desired finished product. Sometimes chunks of recycled glass called cullet are added to the mixture. Coloring agents are also added and include iron (green, blue, and yellow), cobalt (blue), gold (ruby red), iron and copper (black), and nickel (deep blue to violet).

It can take thirty to sixty minutes to heat the batch to a red-hot liquid state. After the glass ingredients are molten, the pot is removed from the furnace and allowed to cool. This hazardous operation, called pot changing, is described by Peter Layton in *Glass Art:*

> Pot-changing . . . is one of the most dramatic sights imaginable. A furnace may contain several pots and cannot therefore be allowed to cool, so the operation has to be carried out rapidly, at high temperatures. Figures completely swathed in protective clothing and starkly illuminated by the glare of the furnace evoke a scene of medieval torture and sorcery.[22]

Glassblowing

To begin making a piece of glass art, the gaffer must dip an iron blowpipe into the crucible where the cooling glass has the consistency of thick syrup. After a ball of glass is rolled onto the blowpipe, several steps are necessary to shape and

This glass blower, or gaffer, gently blows into an iron blow pipe to inflate a piece of molten glass into a large globe.

build the piece. First, the ball of glass is carried to a marver, a flat heatproof surface, usually a polished steel slab. The glass is rolled from side to side on the marver until it lengthens into the desired shape. If necessary, the gaffer will return to the pot stove to add more layers of molten glass to build a thicker piece.

The next step involves shaping the piece of cooling glass with metal tongs called jacks that form the glass in a way that a potter might use the hands to form a piece of clay. This is done in a bottle-maker's chair, a workbench with long arms on which the blowpipe may be rolled back and forth. Another method of shaping glass involves rolling it in a wooden ladle called a block. During shaping, glass cools quickly and needs to be reheated, sometimes fifty or sixty times, in a small, extremely hot gas-fired oven called a glory hole.

GLASS ETCHING

A piece of glass art may be decorated in a number of ways. Etching, a technique developed in the nineteenth century, involves applying wax or a self-adhesive vinyl or rubber sheet, called a resist, to the glass. A design is traced on the resist and cut out with a stencil knife. Areas that are not to be etched are covered with the resist. For chemical glass etching, a paste made from hydrofluoric acid is applied. This substance eats away the glass and leaves a frosted pattern. The acid fumes are extremely toxic to lungs and skin. Glass etchers need to wear protective eyewear, respirators, and rubber boots, gloves, and aprons.

A safer and more widely used technique involves sandblasting. Glass artists who sandblast cover the surface of the glass with a blasting resist, place the glass in a blasting cabinet, and blast the pattern with a sandblaster attached to an air compressor. The sandblaster sprays silicon carbide onto the glass, which abrades and roughens it, leaving a design.

After the piece is shaped lines, circles, and other patterns of colors can be added to the outside. Gaffers purchase glass colors in the form of powders, granules, fragments, shards, or soft glass rods that may be added to the outside of the piece. These are either sprinkled on the marver as the piece is rolled or melted directly onto the surface of the piece. After the glass has taken the desired form and color, a flexible plastic blowhose is attached to the end of the blowpipe. The gaffer gently blows into the hose and slowly inflates the piece, now called a parison. Once the desired shape has been formed, another tube called a punty or punt rod is fused to the bottom of the piece with a piece of molten glass. The blowpipe is cut from the parison with the jacks and remains attached to the punty. To open up the piece or spread the mouth of the glass into a desired shape, jacks are inserted into the neck while the glass is spun.

When a gaffer is finished working with a piece of glass, he or she will place the work of art in a warm kiln for several hours. This allows the glass to cool slowly without cracking or shattering.

Those who practice the arts of glassblowing and ceramics perform tasks that would be familiar to artists of the distant past. In doing so they risk burns, cuts, and other injuries. However, the pieces created with intense heat in an industrial setting can be everlasting and dramatically reflect elements of the earth, fire, and light. In so doing, glass and ceramics can convey a sense of joy and wonder for many years after their creation.

The Photographic Arts

4

In the long history of the visual arts, photography is a relatively new discipline. The first grainy, blurry experimental photos were taken in 1826 by French inventor Joseph Nicéphore Niépce. However, the first practical use of photography was not developed until 1839 when French artist and chemist Louis-Jacques Daguerre invented the method he called the daguerreotype. This process involved coating a mirror plate inside a camera with photosensitive silver halide particles and exposing them to an image for ten to twenty minutes.

Because of the long exposure times, the first photographs were of buildings, but improvements to camera lenses and chemical formulas reduced exposure times to a matter of a few seconds by the 1840s. This allowed photographers to take portraits, and, for the first time, people of the middle class could preserve their images for future generations without paying for expensive paintings. The demand for photographic portraiture quickly escalated, and by 1853 there were at least eighty-six daguerreotype galleries in New York City alone, some producing as many as a thousand portraits a day.

In the following decades photographic methods continued to improve, and many photographers chose to use their cameras to express creative visions. These concepts were based on rules of artistic composition that had been perfected by painters during the Renaissance. It was believed that each photograph should have a center of interest, the main subject should be slightly off center, the horizon should be straight, and the background should be free of distracting objects. In laying down these rules, artist and photographer Myles Birket Foster wrote in 1869 that his goal was "to set forth the laws which govern . . . the arrangement of a picture, so that it shall have the greatest amount of pictorial effect, and to illustrate by examples those broad principles . . . [that] rise to the dignity of art."[23]

Creating art with a camera, however, was no easy task. Some photographers first drew sketches of their intended photograph and then set about the job of assembling models, creating backdrops, and formulating exposure times. Sometimes a photograph was pieced together in a darkroom from several negatives. Commenting on these techniques, painter and photographer Henry Peach Robinson told an apprentice in 1869:

This grainy, blurry picture, taken with an exposure time of eight hours, is the world's first photograph. It was captured in 1826 by Joseph Nicéphore Niépce.

This famous photograph, taken in 1882 by Henry Peach Robinson, shows Englishwomen enjoying an amusing story while taking a break from field work.

"Any dodge, trick, and conjuration of any kind is open to the photographer's use. . . . It is his . . . aim to elevate his subjects, to avoid awkward forms, and to correct the unpicturesque."[24]

Elements of the Camera

From Robinson's time to the present, millions of photographers have endeavored to best use their tools to create fine art. While some have used dodges and tricks to achieve that end, others have captured a moment, made a social statement, or preserved a passing image of beauty with an instant click of the shutter. The tools of photography, like the pigments and brushes of a painter, can produce high quality archival prints that fulfill the artistic vision of the photographer.

The photographer's main tool is the camera, and every nondigital camera consists of four elements. The camera body is a light-tight box that acts as a base for the other elements. The film holder secures sheets or rolls of film to a flat plane opposite the lens. The lens forms an image that is projected onto the surface of the film. (Digital cameras create images electronically and store them on a computer chip, thus eliminating the need for film.)

The fourth element of a camera, the shutter, is a mechanical device that quickly opens and closes when the exposure button is pressed. Shutter speeds are measured in fractions of a second and can be adjusted for a variety of needs. For example, to photograph planets and stars as they move across the dark night sky, a shutter might be left open for several minutes. At the other extreme, some cameras have shutter speeds of 1/8000 that can photograph a drop of water exploding as it hits the ground. Typical cameras have top shutter speeds from 1/1000 to 1/2000, meaning that they can be used to take stop-action photos at sporting events. An average choice for a portrait photograph taken in bright sunlight is 1/125.

The Camera Body

There are several types of camera bodies. The oldest style, variously called a view camera, large-format camera, or studio camera, has changed little since the nineteenth century, and modern view cameras are often mistaken for antiques. The bodies of these cameras consist of a flexible bellows in the midsection, attached to a device called a rear standard that holds a sheet of film. At the front of the camera the lensboard holds the lens in place. To control the focus and perspective of an image, the photographer moves the lensboard closer or farther from the film in the rear standard.

View cameras are large and cumbersome and usually need to be mounted on a tripod, an adjustable three-legged stand. Before taking a picture the operator opens the shutter on the lens. This projects the image onto a glass plate on the rear standard. The photographer can then frame the picture as desired by

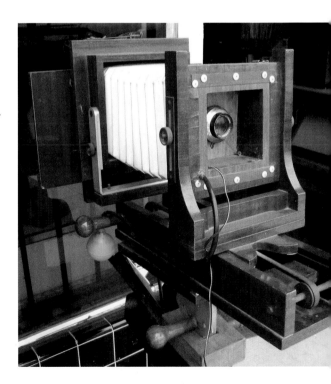

This photo of a view camera shows the lensboard at the front, the flexible bellows behind it, and the rear standard where sheets of film are placed.

moving the tripod and camera and sharply focus the image by moving the lensboard.

After the photo is framed and focused, the photographer needs to select the film exposure by choosing a shutter speed and adjusting the aperture—a ring of overlapping thin metal blades inside the lens. Photographers change aperture settings by turning a ring on the barrel of the lens that is numbered with f-stops (the f stands for focal length). The smaller the f-stop number, the larger the opening on the lens. For example, f/2 is a large aperture opening, while f/22 is small.

The aperture has two main functions. It controls the amount of light that hits the film and it gives a photo what is called depth of field by regulating which objects are in focus. If a photographer wants to take a picture of a person sitting nearby but wants the background of the photo to be blurry, he or she will use f/2, or a large aperture opening. To make the background in focus, the photographer will use f/22 or a small aperture opening. Oftentimes aperture settings are determined with the help of a light meter, a device used to measure the intensity of light that hits the film.

To finally snap the picture, the photographer removes the glass plate, which is held in a metal frame, and inserts in its

A photographer wishing to create a photo like this one with a sharply focused subject and a blurred background uses a large aperture opening.

place a light-tight film holder that contains a sheet of unexposed film. The front of the film holder, called the dark side, is removed and the photographer clicks the shutter, taking the photograph. The dark side is replaced and the film is removed from the camera.

View cameras are generally built for sheet film, and this stock comes in various sizes, always measured in inches, including 4 x 5, 5 x 7, 8 x 10, 11 x 14, 12 x 20, 20 x 24, and 30 x 40. The most popular formats, however, are 4 x 5 and 8 x 10, with the majority of view cameras designed to work with one size or the other.

There are several advantages to the view camera. It provides great precision over the composition and focus of a photograph. In addition, large sheets of film have a much better optical quality than small films typically found in smaller cameras. View cameras can be burdensome, however, as renowned photographer Ansel Adams explains:

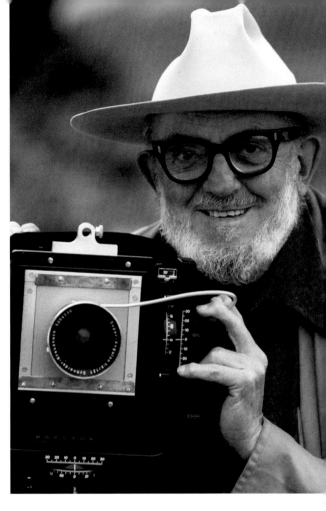

Celebrated photographer Ansel Adams, seen here with a high-quality large-format camera, is recognized as one of the world's greatest nature photographers.

> There is no question that using a view camera requires some physical stamina. In my early years [in the late 1920s] I backpacked through the mountains with an 8 x 10 view camera, two lenses, twelve double film holders, tripods . . . etc. I finally resorted to using pack animals on the trails, and gradually reduced the weight of my equipment. Now, when asked what camera I use, I reply, "The heaviest one I can carry!" Obviously, this is not the camera . . . for casual snapshots, but I believe that the greater effort and restrictions lead to precision of seeing.[25]

The 35mm Camera

Adams has taken many stunning photographs, such as "The Tetons—Snake River," with a view camera. However, it is easy to make mistakes with a large-format camera when focusing and selecting shutter speeds and aperture settings. For this reason many photographers prefer the simplicity of single-lens reflex (SLR) cameras, also called 35mm cameras for the size of the film used.

Thirty-five millimeter cameras use roll film sold in metal canisters called cassettes. When loaded into the camera, the film is secured on a spool, guide tracks, and a pressure plate that keeps it flat. On the outside of the camera body a lever advances the film after it has been exposed, while a rewind knob allows it to be wrapped back onto the cassette when the roll is finished. Many newer cameras have motorized drives that advance and rewind the film.

The 35mm allows what is called through-the-lens (TTL) viewing, which means the photographer is seeing the exact image as it will be captured on film. When using a TTL system the photographer views the image on a moveable mirror that is located between the lens and the film inside the camera body. The photographer can look through the eyepiece and turn the focusing ring on the lens to bring the image into focus. The operator may also turn the aperture ring to adjust the true depth of field. When the photographer presses the shutter release button, the mirror automatically moves away, the shutter opens, and the image is projected through the lens onto the film.

Modern-style SLR cameras were first produced in Japan by Pentax, Canon, Nikon, and Yashica in the late 1950s. The through-the-lens viewing available in these cameras eliminated many of the mistakes common to photographers, such as taking an out of focus picture, setting the wrong exposure, or even forgetting to remove the lens cap. The relative small size of the camera and its ease of use made 35mms the choice for millions of photographers by the end of the 1960s. As Tom and Michele Grimm write in *The Basic Book of*

ANSEL ADAMS

Ansel Adams (1902–1984) is recognized as one of the world's greatest nature photographers. According to his biography on the Sierra Club Web site, Adams also used his photographs to preserve and protect the wilderness:

[*A*nsel Adams] is seen as an environmental folk hero and a symbol of the American West, especially of Yosemite National Park. Adams' dedication to wilderness preservation . . . [and] his signature black-and-white photographs inspire an appreciation for natural beauty and a strong conservation ethic. . . .

Ansel Adams . . . first visited Yosemite in 1916 . . . [and] was transfixed by the beautiful valley. . . . Adams' interest in photography grew and often brought him up to the mountains accompanied by a mule laden with photographic gear and supplies. . . . Adams' role in the Sierra Club grew rapidly and the Club became vital to his early success as a photographer. . . . Adams' images were first used for environmental purposes when the Sierra Club was seeking the creation of a national park in the Kings River region of the Sierra Nevada. Adams lobbied Congress for a Kings Canyon National Park . . . and created an impressive, limited-edition book, *Sierra Nevada: The John Muir Trail,* which influenced . . . President Franklin Roosevelt to embrace the Kings Canyon Park idea. The park was created in 1940.

Sierra Club, "Ansel Adams & the Sierra Club," 2006. www.sierraclub.org/ansel_adams/ about.asp.

Photography, these cameras allowed nearly anyone to take artistic photos:

If there is anything in photography's history that was especially responsible for helping cameras become an exciting part of today's creative society, it was the introduction of the 35mm camera. Modern . . . SLR cameras are the favorites of most amateur and professional photographers. And for good reasons. They are versatile, durable, economical, and produce exceptional results.[26]

Since they were first introduced, 35mm cameras have continued to be improved. By the early 1970s built-in through-the-lens light meters enabled photographers to accurately set the aperture and shutter speed. In the mid-1980s autofocus systems were introduced that automatically focused the image. In the 1990s advances in digital technology and micromotors allowed camera manufacturers to add a host of new features. Sophisticated autoexposure systems measure the light that enters the film chamber and automatically close the shutter when the film is properly exposed. Autoflash systems turn on a built-in flash when the autoexposure system determines that existing light is too low for a proper exposure. Autoload and autorewind systems automatically thread, advance, and rewind film.

The 35mm camera changed the history of photography with its versatility, durability, and ease of use.

Lenses: The Heart of the Camera

Photographers who work with 35mm cameras have a wide variety of lenses that can be removed and interchanged depending on the desired outcome. Camera lenses are manufactured in many shapes and styles but all perform the same basic function: They act as a magnifying glass that forms an image that is projected onto the surface of the film. Because the lens is the sole object between the image and the film, it is considered to be an extremely important tool. As John P. Schaefer advises photographers in *An Ansel Adams Guide: Basic Techniques of Photography:* "The lens is really the heart of a camera, and the lens you choose and the way you use it will, to a great extent, be limiting factors in determining the quality of the photographs you produce."[27]

Photographers choose their lenses depending on the subject of the photo. To capture an image of an object that is far away, a photographer will use a telephoto lens. To take a picture of the widest possible view, the photographer will use a wide-angle lens. Telephoto lenses are long, up to 500mm, while wide-angle lenses are short, about 28mm. Lenses used for general photography are usually 55mm.

Many lenses used today, called zoom lenses, cover a range of focal lengths in a single lens. For example, a 35mm to 70mm zoom lens allows photographers to shoot pictures anywhere between a minimum wide angle (35mm) and a minimum telephoto (70mm) without changing lenses. Other types are called telezooms, or telephoto zoom lenses, and allow a photographer to zoom in to distant objects. A typical telezoom will be 80mm to 200mm. Wide-angle zooms such as the 17mm to 35mm are also available. The most versatile zoom is the 28mm to 105mm.

Color and Black-and-White Film

If lenses are the heart of the camera, film is the canvas on which the photographer records his or her art, and the type of film used in a picture can affect the final result. With more than 125 types of 35mm roll film available, photographers have a wide assortment to choose from; however, there are

When a photographer snaps a shutter to take a picture, light strikes the film in the camera and records the image seen through the lens. However, photographic film is sensitive to certain types of light that are invisible to the human eye. For this reason photographers may use optical filters to alter the light that hits film or photo paper.

Several standard types of optical filters are commonly used in both color and black-and-white photography. Ultraviolet (UV) filters are often kept on a camera at all times. These not only protect the lens from scratches and other damage, but cut down on UV light that creates a noticeable visual haze on photographs taken outdoors.

A polarizing filter has a similar effect as polarized sunglasses, eliminating glare and harsh reflections on bright sunny days. These filters dramatically highlight clouds and darken a blue sky.

A third type of filter, called a neutral density (ND) filter, does not alter light but simply reduces the level of light hitting the film. These gray filters are used to shoot high-speed film on a sunny day or to allow the photographer to use a wider lens opening to create a shorter depth of field.

Ultraviolet optical filters like the one on this lens limit UV light that creates a noticeable haze on outdoor photographs.

three main types of film in general use. Color print film creates a negative in the camera that is used to make paper and digital prints. Color film first became available to the general public in the late 1950s, and today about 95 percent of all film sold in the United States is this type.

A type of color film commonly called slide film does not make a negative. Instead, the film creates a color positive. After being developed this film is mounted on a plastic or cardboard frame, called a slide, that can be projected onto a screen with a slide projector. This type of film is often used by professionals taking pictures for publication and by artists who wish to create slide shows from a number of pictures.

Black-and-white film creates a negative from which black-and-white prints can be made. This film is often used by newspaper photographers who do not require color. It is also a popular choice for art photos because it reveals images in pleasing shades of gray, black, and white.

Photographers shooting in color or black-and-white film often select film based on its sensitivity to light. Manufacturers label their products with what is called an ISO (International Standard for Organization) number. Film that is used in bright sunlight is less sensitive and is called slow-speed film. Film that is extremely light sensitive is called high-speed film. Slow-speed film is rated ISO 25 to 50, medium-speed film is ISO 64 to 200, high-speed film is ISO 400 to 3200.

Film Speeds

Each film speed has its own advantages. Slow-speed films produce the best quality photographs, with sharp images and vivid colors, because slow-speed film is coated with a minimum of light-sensitive particles. High-speed film allows the photographer to use a faster shutter speed and a smaller aperture to achieve greater depth of field. However, because they are coated with a larger amount of light-sensitive particles than slow-speed film, pictures taken with high-speed film tend to be grainy. To achieve a compromise, many photographers choose medium-speed films, which are relatively fast and relatively low grain.

Slides like the one shown on this lightbox are made from film that creates a positive, rather than negative, image.

A type of medium-speed film called infrared is used by photographers who wish to create unpredictable, artistic photos with otherworldly color effects. Infrared film registers invisible infrared radiation as well as visible-light and produces astonishingly distorted colors in a photograph. Depending on the type of filters used, trees and grass may appear vivid pink, magenta, and red; the sky might be green; and a human face can photograph as deep blue.

Darkroom Tools

Shooting film in a camera is the first phase of a three-part process. The second is developing the negatives, and the third is printing the images. Some photographers prefer to perform the second and third phases themselves. To do so, they set up darkrooms, often in bathrooms, basements, kitchens, spare rooms, garages, or even large closets. With a few relatively inexpensive tools the photographer can manipulate his or her images to create artistic prints. However, because of the technical difficulties involved in developing color prints, most darkroom photographers prefer to work only with black-and-white film.

The first requirement of a darkroom is that it be absolutely dark, since film is ruined by exposure to light during the first

Developing Photos in a Darkroom

1. When processing film, the film is rolled onto a plastic reel (front) in total darkness before it is placed in a light-tight film-developing tank (rear).

2. Chemicals such as these are used to develop and fix film and photographic papers.

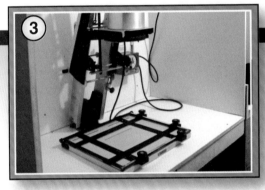

3. Finished negatives are placed in the enlarger (top). Photographic paper is placed in the easel (bottom) and exposed for a short period of time.

4. Photographers may choose from a variety of photographic papers that vary in contrast, speed, finish, and size.

5. Once exposed, photographic paper is placed in trays like these that contain developer, stop bath, fixer, and a water wash.

6. After the print is exposed, the paper may be dried in a print dryer like this one.

part of the development process. Any windows and cracks around doors must be covered with heavy black paper, Styrofoam and black duct tape, or blankets. Running water at a controlled temperature is another necessity for darkroom work. While some photographers make do with kitchen sinks or bathtubs, others prefer specially designed large, flat darkroom sinks.

The first steps for processing 35mm film are done in total darkness. The photographer removes the long roll of film from the metal cassette with a film cartridge opener. The film is coiled onto a special metal or plastic reel that is then placed in a light-tight film-developing tank. Lights may be turned on after this step is completed.

Developing film involves three chemicals. Developer forms the image on the film; stop bath, made from acetic acid, stops the development process; and fixer makes the image permanent, or fixes it, on the film. The chemicals are sold as concentrated liquids or powders and are mixed in plastic bottles. During the development process the chemicals must be used at specific temperatures between 65° and 75°F (18° to 24°C). This requires a photographer to use a special thermometer. The amount of time the film is in the developer is also important, and large clocks called interval timers, with a range of one second to sixty minutes, are necessary items in any darkroom.

After the film is developed it is washed with water and treated with a few drops of a wetting agent that prevents water spots on the negative. The film is taken off the reel, excess water is removed with a squeegee, and the film is hung up to dry with a clothespin. When the film is dry, scissors are used to cut the long strip into short pieces that are easier to handle.

Tools for Printing

The second part of the developing process involves printing the picture on photographic paper. Since black-and-white photographic paper is not sensitive to red light waves, a red lamp called a safe light is used to illuminate the darkroom during printing.

LIGHTING AND FLASH

The word "photography" is taken from the Greek word *photographia*, meaning "light writing," and most photographers prefer to take pictures using natural light. However, people who need to take pictures indoors or at night can use a variety of artificial illumination. Professionals who work in a photo studio light their subjects with lamps that use very bright tungsten bulbs called hot lights. Hot lights, mounted on light stands, come in many styles, including spotlights, and projection spotlights.

To soften the harsh effects created by hot lights, photographers use an assortment of reflectors called bounces, diffusers, and deflectors. Foremost among these are studio umbrellas, made from highly reflective silver material. Studio umbrellas can bounce light toward—or reflect light away from—a subject.

Professional and amateur photographers also rely on flash attachments, which provide a momentary burst of bright light while the camera shutter is open. Most 35mm and digital cameras are sold with a battery-powered built-in flash. Another type of flash, called a handle-mount flash, is attached to the camera with a long cord but may be held away from the camera by the operator to take well-lit portraits of large groups of people at weddings and other events.

To expose paper to the image on a negative, the photographer uses an enlarger that consists of a light source, a lens with an aperture, a negative carrier, a baseboard, and support system that holds the enlarger head. A paper holder called an easel is placed on the baseboard under the enlarger lens. The negative is loaded onto the negative carrier and placed between the light source and the lens. To focus the image on the easel the light source is switched on and the enlarger head is moved up or down on the support. When the image is focused, photographic paper is placed on the easel. The enlarger is connected to the interval timer so that when the source light is turned on, it shines through the negative on the paper for a specific number of seconds, and then clicks off automatically.

The paper is then ready to be developed using a method similar to that of developing negatives. The exposed paper is placed sequentially in four trays containing developer, stop bath, fixer, and a water wash. These large, flat plastic trays can accommodate papers that average 8 x 10 inches and can be as big as 11 x 14 inches. After the paper is washed it may be dried in a print dryer or left to dry on a drying rack.

Although the photographic process is one of chemicals, films, and exacting times, the camera has the unique ability to record what the human eye can see. For some, this transformation of a living image into a permanent photo is a magical process unlike any other art. And the millions of photographs taken by amateurs and professional photographers each year have created a living historical record that will entertain, amuse, and educate future generations for many years to come.

Digital and Computer Art

Computers have revolutionized nearly every aspect of life since the late 1980s. While most people use computers for education, entertainment, communication, and shopping, visual artists have adapted digital technology in pursuit of creative expression. Using scanners, cameras, software, and traditional painting and drawing materials, artists are using the computer as a twenty-first-century canvas. In doing so, these artists have made digital art one of the most vibrant art forms today. Commenting on this phenomenon, Rachel Greene, founder of Rhizome.org, a digital art Web site, states:

> Digital art reflects the way we live now in a technological culture. . . . If you look at landscape paintings at the [Metropolitan Museum of Art], in many ways they're nostalgic works because they don't reflect the world we live in. If you're interested in commenting on contemporary life, you have to address communication on the Internet, the information culture, video games.[28]

Programming Computers

Digital art may consist of photo art, drawn and painted art, algorithmic and fractal art, mathematical art, and a kaleidoscopic

Basic tools for a digital artist include a computer keyboard, mouse, and display monitor.

combination of other computerized forms. These styles are progressing on an unprecedented scale as sophisticated software and digital technology allow artists an ever-increasing degree of versatility. However, the first digital creators, such as Italian artist and engineer Aldo Giorgini, did not have the tools many take for granted today. In the days before software painting programs and the mouse, Giorgini had to spend long hours programming computers to make simple drawings of concentric circles and other shapes. His methods are described in a 1974 magazine article by Larry Bullock:

> The process of computer-aided drawing requires three steps. First, an idea conceived by the artist must be translated into some useable form. This is accomplished by using mathematical formulae with appropriate parameters that enable the machine to manipulate the human concepts. Secondly, the formulae must be expertly programmed into the computer. Lastly, as the computer draws out the desired pattern on an output device, the idea can then be fully implemented by the

artist's intervention or transformed according to any particular whims or innovations that the artist might conceive at the moment. Tedious blackening of desired areas (by hand) creates special effects that emphasize intricate patterns of lines and spaces.[29]

The Computer

Giorgini, who died in 1994, lived long enough to see digital technology move into the modern era, but even equipment available in the early nineties would be considered primitive by

ALDO GIORGINI: COMPUTER ARTS PIONEER

In 1975, computer art pioneer Aldo Giorgini provided the following autobiography to the editor of an art magazine:

My art background is, perhaps, somehow unusual if compared to the average American artist. At the age of ten, I was asked to apprentice to Carlo Ingeneri, a now well-known painter and sculptor of Decamere, Eritrea. . . . Notwithstanding my dedication (I was spending an average of three hours a day in the studio) and my success in handling the media, I never considered seriously a future in art. . . . A realistic assessment of my talents . . . made me choose engineering for a career.

Since entering college I have only occasionally produced some artwork, but the dormant interest woke up four years ago, when I started . . . using the computer as a scientific tool. In the years 1966–67 . . . I made some computer generated movies. . . . Once at Purdue . . . I started "playing around" with some of the computer drawings that were made as illustrations of the research done. From here to the purposeful use of the computer as an art tool the pace was very short.

Aldo Giorgini, "Aldo Giorgini," AtariArchives.org, 2006. www.atariarchives.org/artist/sec3.php.

today's standards. In the twenty-first century artists are limited only by their imaginations as computers continue to evolve.

There are two basic types of computer available to the digital artist, Apple Macintosh and the PC manufactured by a number of companies. Although it makes up less than 10 percent of total sales, the Macintosh has long been the first choice of professional graphic artists and illustrators because Apple has played a leading role in the development of professional multimedia graphics and other software.

Whatever type of computer an artist uses, however, hard drive storage and processor speed are central to effortless creation. Since many art programs use a lot of computer memory, artists need computers with a great deal of RAM, or random access memory, to run them. Individual art pieces can occupy large amounts of disk space, so computer artists also prefer to have hard drives that will store as many gigabytes (GB) as possible. In recent years, however, even the cheapest computers have more than enough hard drive storage for most art projects.

Processor speed allows the computer to perform functions nearly instantaneously so the artist does not have to pause while the computer catches up. Speed is measured in gigahertz (GHz) and, generally speaking, the higher the number the faster the computer. Like hard drive storage, processor speeds continue to increase every year, and any newer computer can meet most demands made by computer artists. In addition, a wide variety of hard drives and processors are available to anyone who wants to upgrade an older model.

For many digital artists, the display monitor is at least as important as the computer. Monitors allow the artist to see his or her creation, and the size and resolution of the display can affect the quality of the artist's work. Because digital artists often need to zoom in on their work, bigger displays are more versatile and easier to use. For example, if a person zooms up to 200 percent, the picture takes up four times more space on

Apple CEO Steve Jobs shows off a thirty-inch, high-resolution display monitor.

the monitor as it does at 100 percent. Large screens also provide more room to display the toolbars, palettes, and dialog boxes that are part of software applications. Although these can be opened and closed as necessary, it is more convenient to leave them open. On small displays, the toolbars alone can take up more room than the artwork.

Size is not the only limiting factor on screen displays. Screen clarity is determined by resolution, the number of pixels that are displayed on the screen (pixels are the colored dots generated by a computer to construct a screen image). The more pixels used to represent an image, the closer it resembles the original. For displays, pixels are expressed as a pair of numbers. For example, the twenty-inch Apple Cinema Display has 1680 x 1050 pixels while the thirty-inch has 2560 x 1600. (In 2005 the highest maximum resolution for any type of monitor was 3840 x 2400 pixels.) Monitors with higher resolution allow artists to see greater detail in their work.

Several types of monitors are available, each with its own advantages and disadvantages. Old style displays called CRT (cathode ray tube) are heavy and large. However, these monitors generate bright pictures with sharp contrast. They are also less expensive compared to newer, LCD (liquid crystal display) technology. In the past, LCD monitors had limited contrast and restricted viewing angles. However, these slim, lightweight units are improving every year and have become the industry standard for graphic artists and illustrators.

Creating Digital Images

Whatever the capabilities of their computers and monitors, the work of digital artists is centered on images. These are either made on the computer or are generated elsewhere and imported onto the hard drive using a variety of commonly available tools.

Photos are an integral part of many styles of digital artwork, including photomontage, photo manipulation, enhanced photography, and assembled photography, or collage. While such artwork may be based on traditional photographs, film cameras are being rapidly replaced by digital cameras. In 2006 more than three quarters of all cameras sold were digital, and digital images accounted for 70 percent of all professionally taken photographs.

Digital cameras have built-in computers that record images on semiconductors that turn the images into digital data. The cameras are rated by the number of megapixels they can record in a photo. Cameras with higher megapixel numbers cost more but can take photos with better resolution that provide more detail. These can be printed in larger sizes without losing quality. In 2006 a 3-megapixel camera could be purchased for less than one hundred dollars, while 9-megapixel cameras averaged around four hundred dollars. At the high end of the scale, a Nikon D2X 12.4-megapixel camera cost around three thousand dollars not including the lens.

Digital cameras are also rated according to their internal memory, or ability to store photos, and most do not have a high memory capacity. Cheaper 3-megapixel digital cameras offer as little as 8 MB (megabytes)—enough to store only about sixty pictures. Photographers who wish to store more pictures must purchase memory cards that may hold from 16 MB to over 1 GB of photographic information.

Digital photographers also need to consider lenses. While cheaper models have fixed lenses for general photography, art photographers require versatility, and many prefer cameras with zoom lenses that go from wide angle to telephoto. A common lens called a 10x zoom provides this flexibility, equal to a nondigital 28mm to 300mm zoom lens.

In 2006, more than three-quarters of all cameras sold were digital models like this Canon 20d.

Scanners

Images taken with a digital cameras can be downloaded directly onto a computer hard drive. Those shooting film or working with traditionally painted or drawn artwork, however, need to input the images with a scanner. Like cameras, scanners record images in pixels and are rated by the quantity of pixels they can record with their image sensors. This number is often stated in dots per inch (dpi) or pixels per inch (ppi) and higher numbers correspond with better resolution.

There are two basic types of scanners, flatbed and film scanners. Flatbeds are the most common and most versatile because they can scan photos, drawings, paintings, printed works, and even objects. These scanners are inexpensive, and even the cheapest models can scan up to 1440 dpi. However, most scanners are limited by their scanning areas of about 9 x 12 inches (23 x 30cm). Artists who wish to scan larger images must use wide-format flatbed scanners that are about twice that size. These scanners cost several thousand dollars, though, so those who need to scan large pieces often pay to have them digitized at professional graphics studios instead.

Artists who wish to scan photographic slides or film negatives can purchase flatbed scanners with transparency adapters

Flatbed scanners are used by computer artists to digitize images from photos, drawings, paintings, printed works, and even objects.

that project light through the film to record the image. However, these adapters are less effective than dedicated film scanners that are specially made for slides and negatives. A good film scanner with an 1800 dpi can be purchased for about one hundred dollars while 4000 dpi scanners may cost up to four hundred dollars.

Painting, Drawing, and Modeling

However they are produced, digital images are stored as files on a computer's hard drive. These can be manipulated and combined in an infinite variety of ways with software designed for photography, drawing, painting, or 3D modeling. This software is divided into three basic categories: bitmap painting, vector drawing, and 3D modeling.

Bitmap illustration, or image editing software, breaks images down into pixels, and each pixel may be one of 16 million different colors. Artists using bitmap-based photo and illustrations programs such as Adobe PhotoShop, Corel Photo-Paint, and Jasc Paint Shop Pro can create marks on their work as if they were using a paintbrush and canvas. They can also merge the painted elements with photographs.

Painting software is extremely sophisticated and allows artists to work with digital colored pencils, watercolors, and oil brushes, using colors based on real paints. Mixing palettes let artists blend their own colors as well. This software also allows the artist to control the amount of oil, viscosity, color blend, brush texture, and color thickness seen on the screen. Corel Painter even enables each brush dab to hold a finite amount of oil and as the oil runs out, the brush stroke becomes fainter. Painting software also lets artists instantly transform a photo into a painting.

A second type of software, called vector drawing, uses mathematical calculations to create images such as rectangles, squares, polygons, and smooth curves. These programs, including Adobe Illustrator, Corel DRAW, and Macromedia Free Hand are used by artists who wish to build pieces from

FRACTALS AND DIGITAL ART

Fractals, or geometric patterns that are repeated to produce irregular shapes, play an important role in digital art. This subject is explored by J.D. Jarvis:

In the mid '70s, [a] seminal moment in the development of digital image making occurred when mathematician Benoit Mandelbrot brought to attention what he called "Fractal Geometry." Mandelbrot . . . was able to show how these infinitely repeatable mathematical forms [fractals] occur in what was often considered random or free-flowing structures within nature. While working at IBM's Watson Research Center [in New York], he had developed some of the first computer programs to print graphics. He used these facilities to demonstrate how his fractal geometry could describe complex natural forms, such as cloud formations, the distribution of leaves and twigs on a tree, the shape of a coastline, or the infinitely self-[repeating] form of a seashell. In combination, fractal mathematics and digital computing brought a new kind of image to art making. Patently beautiful and seductive, fractal images seem to display the math of the infinite.

Joseph Nalven and J.D. Jarvis, "Going Digital: The Practice and Vision of Digital Artists," MOCA: Museum of Computer Art, July, 2005. http://moca.virtual.museum/editorial/jdgoingdigital.htm.

simple elements and combine them into finished drawings that include illustrations, text, colors, fills, and images. The advantage of working with vector objects is that they are easy to change, edit, and print.

3D Modeling

While vector and bitmap applications can be compared with drawing or painting on paper, 3D modeling is more like carving a sculpture from stone. Artists working with 3D software, such as Adobe 3D, Bryce, Cool 3D, and Poser can build three-dimensional models and arrange them in a virtual world to create unique and sophisticated science fiction and fantasy-based pieces. However, 3D imaging is complex and time-consuming and often requires the artist to work with several software programs in order to execute a vision. Dutch 3D artist Kees Roobol describes his creative process:

> An image usually starts fairly finished in my head. . . . Since most if not all of my textures are photographic, PhotoShop is the first application to work with. . . . Poser is a nice tool too, but I mostly use it to experiment with different poses in draft versions. For the final render I prefer [photos of] real humans; these can be friends, neighbors or actors at historical reconstructions or in historical museums. . . . In the second phase, the entire scene is built in Bryce. . . . And of course, once I have finished, the resemblance to the original idea is usually only marginal. . . . About 100–150 hours of work for a single image are not exceptional, hence my productivity of 5–6 images per year.[30]

The Graphics Tablet

Whether working with 3D or simpler drawing programs, artists often find that it can be difficult to manipulate digital images using a standard mouse. For some, an optical mouse, which uses a light-emitting diode to detect movement, provides a greater degree of accuracy than the moving parts of a mechanical mouse. Others prefer a trackball mouse, which consists of a ball, housed in a socket, that can be manipulated to move the cursor.

Most professional artists, however, prefer to work with a graphics tablet, a device that allows artists to hand-draw images directly onto a computer, rather than by using a mouse. The graphics tablet, also referred to as a digitizing tablet, graphics pad, or drawing table, consists of a pressure-sensitive stylus that can be used to draw upon the flat surface of the device's

tablet. The image does not appear on the tablet but rather on the computer display. Some styli are sold with erasing ends that allow artists to delete mistakes.

Tablets react to the pressure and tilt of the stylus in the artist's hand, providing a high degree of control over line thickness, transparency, and color. Most tablets have either 256, 512, or 1024 levels of pressure and the higher the number the easier it is for the artist to control the software tools by changing how hard he or she presses the pen tip to the tablet surface.

Graphics tablets are sold in various sizes ranging from 4 x 5 inches (10 x 13cm) to more expensive 12 x 18-inch (30.5 x 46cm) tablets. The larger the tablet surface, the more the artist needs to move his or her hands and arms. While some favor a smaller tablet to minimize arm motion, artists who commonly paint or draw with large sweeping motions prefer a larger tablet.

Storing Digital Art

Unlike a painter who fills the walls of a studio with dozens of finished canvases, digital artists can store hundreds of pieces of art on a computer hard drive or CD. CDs are the cheapest storage method, and a single CD, which can be purchased for less than fifty cents, can hold up to seven huge, 100-MB PhotoShop files or hundreds of smaller files saved in the JPEG format. Many computers are sold with built-in CD burners, and dozens of external CD burners are available for under one hundred dollars.

Displaying Digital Art

Most artists wish to show their work to others, and those working with computers have many options for display. Art can be viewed on a computer monitor, posted on the Web, or e-mailed to others. Some artists prefer to print hard copies of their work, and these may be hung on a wall like traditional paintings.

To create hard copies, an artist needs a good printer, and there are many models available. Most fall into two categories, ink-jet or laser-jet. Although ink-jet printers are cheaper, many believe that they produce the best-quality pictures. When used with high-quality photographic paper, ink-jet images can be favorably compared to film photographs. Printers are often limited by size, however, and most can print images only a little larger than 8.4 x 14 inches (21 x 35cm). Artists who want to print large pieces up to 46 inches (117cm) wide can purchase a large-format printer that costs between twenty-five hundred dollars and forty-five hundred dollars. Those wishing to avoid this expense can have their work printed at commercial graphics studios that charge around ten dollars per square foot.

Digital art may be stored on a variety of formats including CDs.

The installation *Listening Post,* by Mark Hansen and Ben Rubin, is viewed by a patron at the Ars Electronica 2004, a digital arts festival in Linz, Austria.

The newest type of printer is a dedicated photo printer. While most people use photo printers to make prints from their digital cameras, these printers can also be used by artists who wish to create high quality prints of their work. The disadvantage of photo printers is that most models make prints only up to 4 x 6 inches (10 x 19cm) in size, too small for most digital art shows.

Digital Exhibitions

Artists who wish to exhibit their digital work for the public can post it on the Internet in galleries such as rhizome.org, digitalart.org, and digitalartmuseum.com. These sites provide links to other sites that are created by artists from around the world and feature art, artist statements, and biographies. Many Web sites also offer interactive experiences that allow visitors to change or participate in creating pieces, blurring the boundaries between artist and viewer.

Artists also display their work and collaborate at international digital art festivals such as Ars Electronica in Austria, the Dutch Electronic Arts Festival in the Netherlands, the New York Digital Salon, and the Special Interest Group in Graphics (SIGGRAPH), held in various U.S. cities.

Major museums have recently begun to display digital art. In 2001 the critically acclaimed "010101: Art in Technological Times" show was held at the San Francisco Museum of

INTERNET ART

Artists have long relied on exhibitions, gallery owners, and art critics to validate their work. However, a new generation of digital artists using computers and software have changed the very meaning of art and its worth, as Adrian Shaughnessy explains:

Defining what is and what isn't art used to be easy. Then [French artist] Marcel Duchamp came along and announced that anything —even a urinal—could be art. . . .

And, just as Duchamp did in the early part of the 20th century, Internet art assaults many of our most cherished notions about art. First, art on the Internet is accessible to anyone with a computer and Web connection. This is in sharp contrast to contemporary fine art, which still, even in its most radical guises, exudes an aura of elitism and privilege that comes from its association with galleries and affluent collectors, both public and private. . . .

Second, Internet art relies on computer code and the technological constraints imposed by shared technologies, which means that on-line art is at least partly determined by the technology . . . [However,] through the misuse of technology and software . . . a new generation of Internet artists have demonstrated their value to the culture.

Adrian Shaughnessy, "Digital Art: Code of Aesthetics," *Design Week*, March 30, 2006, p. 21.

Modern Art, and "BitStreams" was held at the Whitney Museum in New York. Private collectors are also purchasing digital art. For example, limited editions of DVDs containing art by Matthew Barney, Bill Viola, and Shirin Neshat are sold for more than one hundred thousand dollars.

Digital artwork is a world away from the first cave paintings made in prehistoric times. And the rapid rate of change in the digital world will soon make today's offerings seem as primitive by comparison. There is some speculation that future digital artists will be able to create works that will surround a viewer with morphing holographic imagery indistinguishable from reality. However, traditional oil paintings and pastel drawings might gain added value in a world overloaded with digital images. Whatever the case, the future of art is in the hands and minds of those learning to create today—and in the imaginations of artists yet unborn.

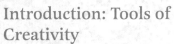

Notes

Introduction: Tools of Creativity

1. Ralph Mayer, *The Artist's Handbook of Materials and Techniques.* New York: Viking, 1991, p. v.
2. Quoted in Michael Delahunt, *Artlex Art Dictionary*, 2006 www.artlex.com.

Chapter 1: Drawing and Painting

3. Quoted in Michael Mark, "Charcoal." www.michaelmark.net/chapter1. html.
4. Angela Gair, ed., *The Artist's Manual.* San Francisco: Chronicle, p. 44.
5. Ray Smith, *New Artist's Handbook.* London: Dorling Kindersley, 2003, p. 9.
6. Quoted in Delahunt, *Artlex Art Dictionary.*
7. Mayer, *The Artist's Handbook,* p. 168.
8. Quoted in James Ayres, *The Artist's Craft: A History of Tools, Techniques, and Materials.* Oxford: Phaidon, 1985, p. 110.
9. Quoted in Gair, *The Artist's Manual,* p. 149.
10. Quoted in Delahunt, *Artlex Art Dictionary.*
11. Gair, *The Artist's Manual,* p. 12.

Chapter 2: Tools of the Sculptor

12. Jack C. Rich, *The Materials and Methods of Sculpture.* New York: Dover, 1988, p. 3.

13. Quoted in Delahunt, *Artlex Art Dictionary.*
14. Oliver Andrews, *Living Materials: A Sculptor's Handbook.* Berkeley and Los Angeles: University of California Press, 1983, p. 117.
15. Andrews, *Living Materials,* p. 247.
16. Quoted in Piero Mussi and Mavis McClure, "Bronze Sculpture: The Art of Lost Wax," Modern Sculpture.com, 2000. www.modernsculpture.com/ bronze.htm.
17. Quoted in Mussi and McClure, "Bronze Sculpture."
18. Andrews, *Living Materials,* p. 274.

Chapter 3: Ceramics and Glass

19. Andrews, *Living Materials,* p. 9.
20. Tony Birks, *The Complete Potter's Companion.* Rev. ed. Boston: Bulfinch, 1998, p. 117.
21. Birks, *The Complete Potter's Companion,* p. 111.
22. Peter Layton, *Glass Art.* Seattle: University of Washington Press, 1996, p. 109.

Chapter 4: The Photographic Arts

23. Quoted in Beaumont Newhall, *The History of Photography.* New York: Museum of Modern Art, 1982, p. 76.
24. Quoted in Newhall, *The History of Photography,* p. 78.

25. Quoted in John P. Schaefer, *An Ansel Adams Guide: Basic Techniques of Photography.* Boston: Little, Brown, 1992, p. 54.

26. Tom Grimm and Michele Grimm, *The Basic Book of Photography.* New York: Plume, 2003, p. 31.

27. Schaefer, *An Ansel Adams Guide,* p. 59.

Chapter 5: Digital and Computer Art

28. Quoted in Julie Mehta, "Programming Digital Art: Despite Technological and Ownership Issues, Galleries Are Connecting with This High-Tech Market," *Art Business News,* December 2003, p. 42.

29. Larry Bullock, "CE Prof. Giorgini Connects Art, Science," *Purdue Exponent,* Thursday, March 14, 1974, p. 2.

30. Kees Roobol, "The Hands of Time," MOCA: Museum of Computer Art, April 14, 2006. http://moca.virtual. museum/roobol/roobol01.htm.

For Further Reading

Books

Alan Buckingham, *Photography*. New York: Dorling Kindersley, 2004. An exploration of photographic equipment, methods, and techniques, including information about digital photography.

Diana Craig, Moira Butterfield, and Lynsy Pinsent, *Art for Children: A Step-by-Step Guide for the Young Artist*. Edison, NJ: Chartwell, 1996. A guide to art with projects and discussions about materials and methods.

Joe DeMaio, Robin Worth, and Dennis Curtin, *The New Darkroom Handbook: A Complete Guide to the Best Design, Construction, and Equipment*. Boston: Focal, 1998. An exploration of studios and darkroom design and construction.

Rosie Dickins, *The Usborne Introduction to Art: In Association with the National Gallery, London*. Tulsa, OK: EDC, 2004. Detailed introduction to the history of art with Internet links about featured artists and examples of their work and works by related artists.

Mary Ellis, *Ceramics for Kids: Creative Clay Projects to Pinch, Roll, Coil, Slam and Twist*. New York: Lark, 2002. Provides an introduction to clay and pottery, with instructions for twenty-five projects using various methods, such as a pinch and coil Japanese tea bowl and a press-molded hanging bird bath.

Gail Gibbons, *The Art Box*. New York: Holiday House, 1998. Describes the many different kinds of tools and supplies that artists use to produce their work.

Ray Smith, *New Artist's Handbook*. London: Dorling Kindersley, 2003. A definitive guide to the visual arts with descriptions of materials, equipment, and techniques and over one thousand full-color illustrations.

Web Sites

Artlex Art Dictionary (www.artlex.com). A comprehensive art dictionary, definitions for more than thirty-six hundred terms used in discussing art, and thousands of supporting images, pronunciation notes, great quotations, and cross-references.

Chihuly (www.chihuly.com). The homepage of the man frequently lauded for revolutionizing the Studio Glass movement with his complex, multipart sculptures and environmental installations.

HistoryWorld.net History of Painting (www.historyworld.net/wrldhis/plain texthistories.asp?groupid=1345&his toryid=ab20). An interactive site that explores the history of art from

Neanderthal times to the nineteenth century, with photos.

MOCA: Museum of Computer Art (http://moca.virtual.museum/index.asp). One of the most heavily-trafficked, comprehensive, and respected computer art museums on the Web, MOCA promotes computer art in its various forms, including 3-D art, fractals, enhanced photography, animation, mixed media, and computer-painted and -drawn art.

Museum of Modern Art (www.moma.org). The Web site of the famed museum in New York has an online collection featuring hundreds of images of drawings, paintings, sculpture, and other art created during the twentieth century.

Index

Picture Credits

Cover: © James Marshall/Corbis

© AFP/Getty Images, 50, 59
© Alison Wright/Corbis, 32
© Archivo Iconigrafico, S.A./Corbis, 23, 31
© Chip East/Reuters/Corbis, 13
© Christie's Images/Corbis, 17, 37
© David Hume Kennerly/Getty Images, 67
© Devon Howard, 42, 43
© Fred Prouser/Reuters/Corbis, 40
© Getty Images, 82, 83
© Gjon Mili/Time & Life Pictures/Getty Images, 47
© Henry Groskinski/Time & Life Pictures/Getty Images, 44
© Hulton Archive/Getty Images, 64
© James L. Amos/Corbis, 48

© Joseph Niepce/Hulton Archive/Getty Images, 63
© Kevin Fleming/Corbis, 54
© Marisa Breyer, 9, 14, 19, 26, 66, 70, 72, 74, 85, 90
© Mark Sampson, 16
Maury Aaseng, 75 (design)
© Peter Beck/Corbis, 35
© Peter Harholt/Corbis, 33
© Photos.com, 22, 24, 39, 51, 53, 80, 86, 91
© Rik Ergenbright/Corbis, 57
© Royalty-Free/Corbis, 20
© Rubra/Reuters/Corbis, 92
© Stuart A. Kallen, 10
© Stuart Kallen/Courtesy of Camera Exposure, San Diego, CA, 65, 75 (all photos)

About the Author

Stuart A. Kallen is the author of more than two hundred non-fiction books for children and young adults. He has written on topics ranging from the theory of relativity to the history of rock and roll. In addition, Mr. Kallen has written award-winning children's videos and television scripts. In his spare time, Stuart A. Kallen is a singer/songwriter/guitarist in San Diego, California.